CHARLES RINGMA

CRY FREEDOM

— with voices from the Third World —

CHARLES RINGMA

CRY FREEDOM

with voices from the Third World

AN ALBATROSS BOOK

© Charles Ringma 1998

Published in Australia and New Zealand by
Albatross Books Pty Ltd
PO Box 320, Sutherland
NSW 2232, Australia
and in the United Kingdom by
Lion Publishing plc
Peter's Way, Sandy Lane West
Oxford OX4 5HG, England

First edition 1998

National Library of Australia
Cataloguing-in-Publication data

Ringma, Charles
Cry freedom with voices from the Third World

ISBN 0 7324 1067 3

1. Christianity and justice — Developing countries — Meditations.
2. Spirituality — Developing countries — Meditations. I. Title.

242.2

Cover and interior illustrations: Michael Mucci
Printed by Kyodo Printing Co. Pte Ltd, Singapore

CONTENTS

CONTENTS

Dedication

———

Dedicated to three Christian communities in mission in the Philippines:

Servants, working with the urban poor in Metro Manila;

Samaritana, ministering to women in prostitution in Quezon City;

and

Sam BAHAYO, serving the rural poor through training and empowerment

———

PREFACE

I CONCEIVED THE IDEA OF WRITING A MEDITATIONAL reader which involved listening to the voices from the Third World from the safety and security of the First World. Had it also been written there, it probably would have turned out to be very different from the book you now have in your hands. This book, instead, has been written in the midst of the struggles and pain and hope and courage of people working for change in the Philippines.

I am particularly grateful for the opportunity of serving on the faculty of the Asian Theological Seminary, Metro Manila, and for the privilege of working with those who serve the urban poor. Above all, I am thankful for the way in which the poor themselves have begun to enrich my life. They have taught me something of hope in the midst of degradation and oppression, and of faith in the midst of tears.

I owe much to John Waterhouse, publisher, and

Ken Goodlet, editor of Albatross Books, for their commitment to this series of devotional books. I am also grateful to Karen McColm and Lea Deseo for the arduous task of typing the manuscript from handwritten notes.

Charles Ringma
Metro Manila, Philippines

INTRODUCTION

TRADITIONALLY, BOOKS ON MEDITATION AND reflection have dealt primarily with the themes of solitude and prayer. As a result, writers on spirituality have often been seen as encouraging a world-denying type of Christianity, a spirituality that focusses on the inner life, but fails to be concerned about the outer world. In the companion volumes, *Seize the Day*, *Dare to Journey* and *Resist the Powers*, I have sought to overcome this popular misunderstanding. Spirituality involves our life with our neighbour as well as with God.

In listening to the voices from the developing world, I have sought to develop further the idea that spirituality belongs to the work of justice and that those involved in the work of evangelism, care and transformation of society on behalf of the poor need to be sustained by a relevant theology and a vibrant spirituality.

It is my hope that the reading of *Cry Freedom* will have a number of outcomes:

- *First*, that it will enhance our appreciation of the rich traditions of theology, spirituality and practical strategies that exist in the Third World.

- *Second*, that it will stimulate us to a more radical reading of the Bible and its themes of liberation.

- *Third*, that it will inform our lifestyle and the practice of our faith so that we become better stewards and more caring servants in the name of Christ.

- *Fourth*, that it will deepen our spiritual lives because we have come closer to the Jesus of the Galilean road, who healed and blessed the poor, and further away from the Christ of the ecclesiastical stained glass window.

Cry Freedom is not meant to inspire a sense of guilt about how little we are doing. Instead, it is a vibrant testimony to the faith and courage of our brothers and sisters in Latin America, Africa and Asia. The campesino, the poor of Latin America, are shining examples of this. From their faith and practice, we can be encouraged to live no longer for ourselves, but to serve the least of these our brothers and sisters in a world where so many are oppressed and so many poor have become the wretched of the earth.

INTRODUCING WRITERS
FROM THE THIRD WORLD

CERTAIN NAMES IMMEDIATELY SPRING TO MIND
when we think of well-known Christians from the
Third World. Mother Teresa. Oscar Romero. Desmond Tutu. Gustavo Gutiérrez. Dom Helder
Camara. Leonardo Boff. Juan Segundo. C. René
Padilla. Vinay Samuel. And there are the myriads
of other voices, most of whom are probably unknown to the reader. While some of these are
scholars, others are practitioners and some are
numbered amongst the poor.

All of these that speak from Latin America,
Africa and Asia have a lot in common. They are
passionately concerned about liberation and justice
and appalled by the oppressive structures that
overwhelm the lives of the poor. They are convinced that God has not only heard the cry of the
poor, but that the Great Liberator has sided with
them against the pharaohs of this world. Many

stress that it is actually the poor that are the brothers and sisters that Christ calls us to serve.

Many other themes are common to the writers from the Third World. The call to serve the poor is not the call simply to give aid. It is first of all the call to join with them in a common journey of life and faith. This call involves a joining together with them, leading to a partnership where all, both the poor and us, are empowered. Thus, for these writers, true faith is never a matter of an easy 'believism', but involves the practice of liberation and service on behalf of the needy.

Moreover, if God sides with the oppressed in their struggle for human dignity, hope and salvation, then the church as God's instrument for societal transformation can do no less. It, too, is called to serve the poor, not only by a few of its valiant daughters and sons, but by its whole life. In other words, the church itself must be a transformed community which demonstrates justice, equality, servanthood and mercy. The church as God's instrument of hope in the world must become the place where rich and poor are reconciled, where barriers are broken down and where all can experience equality in and through the grace of our Lord Jesus Christ.

Sadly, for many of the more conservative readers in the First World, the liberation theologies of the Third World appear to be nothing more than a politicised faith, social practice and activism; a Marxist analysis of social problems; and a radicalism tinged with violence. That this is a serious misreading of the majority of writers from the Third World will become increasingly apparent in the pages of this meditational reader.

It will also become apparent through the voices from the Third World that the preoccupation is not simply with service and social action, but also with prayer, with faith, with hope, with solitude. In fact, many writers from the Third World have focussed on a *spirituality* of liberation which has not only reemphasised the traditional disciplines of the practice of spirituality, but has provided challenging ways of understanding the traditional doctrines of the Christian faith.

From Henri Nouwen's foreword to Segundo Galilea's *The Way of Living Faith: A Spirituality of Liberation*, we are reminded that 'again and again Jesus is presented as the true source for a lived spirituality' and that contemplation and activism are inter-related. Notes Nouwen: 'Neither impatient activism nor complacent pietism have a place in this spirituality of liberation.'

May we attune our hearts to these sometimes strange, but always challenging voices and learn a walk of faith that joins justice with mercy, prayer with activism, community with servanthood, and spirituality with social concern.

January

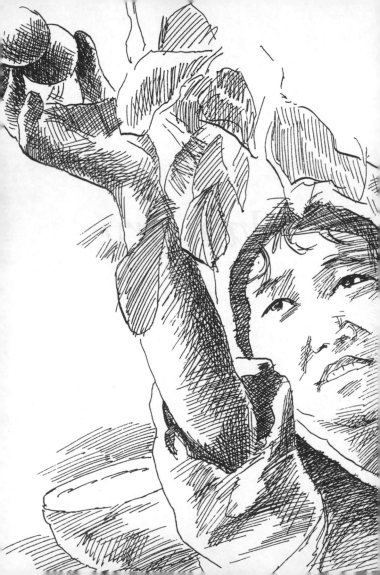

While understanding can lead to particular kinds of actions, the reverse is also true: practical involvement can enrich our understanding.

Theory and practice

'To understand the truth is to do the truth.'
Jon Sobrino

Knowledge and experience are closely related.
It is doubtful whether we really know much
regarding anything of which we have no experience. Similarly, understanding and doing are
intimately connected. While understanding can
lead to particular kinds of actions, the reverse is
also true: practical involvement can enrich our
understanding. Thus, while faith can lead to action,
action will also enrich our faith; and while prayer
can lead to practical engagement, such initiatives
will also deepen our prayers. To sharpen the
focus further, faith that does not lead to action is
probably a spurious faith.

THOUGHT: *Those who seek to understand everything before they act, know little and are probably es-
caping reality. Those who join mind and hand are the
doers who are blessed.*

Prayer and compassion

'O God, to those who have hunger give bread; and
to us who have bread give the hunger for justice.'

A Latin American prayer

Prayer is always a dangerous activity as it has a
way of changing us. Prayer seldom needs to
change the heart of God, for God's interest is already with the poor and suffering. God is already far ahead of us and it is we who have to
catch up with our Redeemer's plans and purposes. Since prayer encourages us to change, it
frequently means that we must put practical action to our own prayers. We cannot pray for the
basics of another's sustenance without also
modifying our lifestyle and responding with
practical compassion.

MEDITATION: *In the cry of the needy, I can hear
God's call to change my ways and work for a more
just society.*

Care in the face of opposition

'In an oppressive society if a group stands up to take care of the lambs, it automatically stands up against the wolves.'

Vishal Mangalwadi

Every society has its powerless members. In the Third World, these are the rural and urban poor. In the First World, these are the ethnic poor, the intellectually disabled, the poorly educated and the permanently unemployed. Whenever the Christian community seeks to do more than provide charity for such groups by working holistically with the poor, it will need to face the issue of injustice. The poor are not just innocent victims. They are not just to be pitied. They are the harassed. They are the marginalised. And they are exploited. Care for them involves changing unjust structures. And help means putting the power of choice into their hands.

MEDITATION: *If we are failing to care for the powerless, we are inadvertently supporting the status quo.*

You have done it to me

'Lord, may I see you today and every day in the person of your sick, and while nursing them, minister to you.'

Mother Teresa

In faith, we who believe acknowledge that the Man from Galilee is the Lord of glory. While this confession may well be appropriate, we need to ensure that we also acknowledge he is present among us. He is with his people in word, sacrament and community. He is also with those whom he is seeking — those who are poor in spirit and those who are poor in resources and possessions. When we minister in love and generosity to any of these groups of people, we also touch the hem of his garment. In serving the members of the community of faith, we serve the body of Christ. In serving the seeker and the powerless, we call them to share in the body of Christ.

PRAYER: *Lord, in serving others in your name, may I touch their pain and need and find your grace and presence there.* Amen.

God and neighbour

'Conversion to God is equally linked to conversion
to the love of neighbour'.

Segundo Galilea

A true turning to God is never an opiate that
guarantees the safety of a future life while leaving us ideologically unchanged. Conversion involves embracing the God who breaks down all
cultural, social and economic barriers. Conversion, therefore, calls us beyond our cultural
prejudices, selfish ambitions and economic self-
seeking into the community of love, acceptance
and sharing. Moreover, it calls us to join our
neighbour in ways that demonstrate the great
love that God has for us. In the embrace of God,
we will not see the sublime without also seeing
the pain of the wretchedness of the earth.

MEDITATION: *Having turned our face to God, we
can truly see the need of our neighbour.*

Sharing

'If there is one area where. . . the first Christian communities sought to make resources available to others, it is in the area of economic sharing.'

Vinay Samuel

The church is not simply a spiritual reality where people are bound together as a communion of souls. The church is also a visible reality where people with social, ethnic and economic differences find a common life in Christ Jesus. Since Jesus is the one who breaks down all barriers which separate and divide people from each other, he also breaks down economic barriers. The common life in Christ Jesus involves a love that gives and a care that shares. Economic sharing is not the discovery of socialism, but the practice of the church filled with the Spirit's love and power.

THOUGHT: *When conversion touches economics the heart has been truly changed.*

Remembering

'The ideology of the dominant classes who have "made it to the top". . . [has] done away with memory in the vanquished.'

Leonardo and Clodovis Boff

Remembering can be a painful but liberating experience. Israel was to remember that God had liberated his people from bondage and oppression in Egypt. The acknowledgment of this fact meant that they should treat others with compassion and justice. However, unlike Israel which could look back to a time of liberation, the people of the First World are not only the perpetrators of oppression, but the practitioners of racial genocide. The near elimination of the American Indians or the Australian Aborigines are stark reminders of this fact. In facing this shameful past, our concern should be that justice be done to the survivors so that their dignity be restored.

THOUGHT: *Someone's dominance has usually come at the cost of another's livelihood and even of life itself.*

Non-violent resistance

'Non-violence laughs at the might of the tyrant and stultifies him by non-retaliation.'

M.K. Gandhi

While violence has long been a part of the practice of the Christian tradition, the example of Christ points us in the opposite direction. He suffered the power of violence and injustice and thereby broke its awesome power. Empowered by the Spirit of Christ, we too can resist the temptation to aggression and retaliation and become peacemakers in our troubled world which so quickly makes use of the gun to solve its political problems. To be a peacemaker, however, does not mean withdrawal and non-involvement. Instead, it means to actively pursue the path of peace even to the point of non-violent resistance and protest which may bring the force of the law on our own heads.

MEDITATION: *To suffer unjustly in the cause of peace is true suffering that will not remain unrewarded.*

Jesus the change agent

'The practice of Jesus is for others; it is meant to change them and to change their world and its relationships.'

Jon Sobrino

While Jesus is the prince of peace, he is also the great disturber. Nothing should remain the same once Jesus has invaded our lives and relationships. If we are changed more and more into being like him, then his concerns become our concerns. And since he desires to make all things new, we too are called to be agents of transformation. As we are changed more and more by his Spirit and our communities of faith are changed, we can become the embodiment of hope and a new way. This new way is not only concerned with spirituality, but also with lifestyle and economics. In fact, its view concerns the whole of life.

PRAYER: *Lord, in the process of changing me, empower me to become an agent of change.* Amen.

Liberation

'The message of the good news is of the liberation of human beings from everything and everyone that keeps them enslaved.'

Elsa Tamez

While we will never experience total freedom in this life, the gospel calls us to embrace the radical freedom that Christ offers. This freedom is both a freedom from the law and from all self-effort to achieve salvation. It is also a freedom from the power of the past and from the stultifying impact of our socialisation. Moreover, it is a freedom from the binding values of our age and from our own drives for security and power. This kind of liberation sets us free for others. It allows us to serve them and to be preoccupied with the work of justice, peace and community building.

THOUGHT: *Freedom always has to be won by over-coming oppressive forces and the death-dealing power of legalism.*

The reality of Christ

'I prefer to let the critics [of the Bible] get on with their own discussions. For my part, I am as sure of Christ's existence as I am of my own hand with its five fingers I can touch and see.'

Dom Helder Camara

Christ is present only to those with faith. But his work in the world is not limited to them. By his Spirit, Christ also draws near to the vulnerable and broken of our world, to those who cry out for God's help and grace, but have not yet come to a personal commitment. Christ is also present in the world of nature, since all things are upheld by his word of power. Little wonder, then, that we can be so sure of Christ's presence. For he is not only in the community of faith, but also in the world upholding and sustaining all things.

PRAYER: *Lord, thank you for the certainty of faith. For all those who struggle with faith's uncertainty, may you bring them comfort, hope and your peace.* Amen.

Those in power

'It is almost impossible to change the people on top merely by preaching, because they are usually happy with the status quo.'

Vishal Mangalwadi

While the powerful enjoy the privileges of their position, they are seldom free enough to respond to the call of their own conscience or to the call of God to walk the narrow way of relinquishment. Showered with adulation and seemingly impenetrable, the powerful are, in fact, vulnerable. For their very strength is their weakness, since they cannot imagine an existence devoid of status and characterised by struggle and pain. Thus, the powerful cling to what they have, regarding such a life as normal and self-evident. Therefore, they know little of the pain of others and of the power of the incarnation, where greatness was reduced to defencelessness in order to demonstrate the way of true power.

THOUGHT: *Power is seldom a virtue. It is more often an oppressive force.*

Possibilities

'Our present situation is beset with difficulties and possibilities.'

Gustavo Gutiérrez

No circumstance is ever wholly negative. Life can be snatched from the jaws of the abyss. In the concrete jungle, green shoots can appear. In the place of oppression, true freedom can be won. But winning such a victory is never without a price. When difficulties become possibilities it is because someone has dared to confront the powers of darkness and has called them to account. When freedom is won in the face of oppression it is because someone has caught a glimpse of the new and has begun to live as if the new is already true.

MEDITATION: *Some only ever see the problems and never see any light. Others are idealists and never face reality. God calls us to live future possibilities in the present.*

Christian community

'It is absolutely imperative that the church be fundamentally a fraternity. If it were anything else, it would lose its relevance in the world'.

Segundo Galilea

Members of the Christian church profess faith in Jesus Christ. They are also called to live a particular quality of life. Central to their lifestyle is the idea that we serve Christ by serving our brothers and sisters and our neighbour whom Christ beckons into fellowship. This service to others is not characterised simply by moments of generosity. It is more basically characterised by economic justice where those who have much and those who have little share so that there may be equality. This demonstrates that Christ has not only changed our souls, but that the awesome power of Mammon has been broken in our lives.

THOUGHT: *In the community of faith, Christ chooses to reveal himself as the one who breaks down the barriers, including that of economic differentiation.*

Renewal

'The Spirit takes hold of persons, fills them with enthusiasm, endows them with special charisms and
abilities to change religion and society, break open
rigid institutions and make things new.'

Leonardo and Clodovis Boff

While one image of the Spirit is that of a peaceful dove, another is that of fire and wind. In the
First World, we prefer the image of the Spirit as
beautifier imparting the fruit of love, peace and
joy. In the Third World, the Spirit is seen as the
liberator. The Spirit empowers with gifts not in
order to make us mature, but in order to make us
change agents. Like Jesus, who in the power of
the Spirit confronted evil and exposed the
hypocrisy of the old order, we also are called to
bring the new into being.

PRAYER: *Holy Spirit, fill me anew with your power
that will enable me to stand for truth and oppose
every form of evil.* Amen.

The future

'The cost of following Jesus entails not only giving up the past, but also giving up various options for the future.'

Vinay Samuel

To give up the past in the following of Jesus is usually no great sacrifice, for our past was marked by folly, waywardness and sin. Giving up particular options regarding our future is another matter. Since we expect our discipleship to lead to blessing, we find it difficult when we discover that it primarily leads to costly service. Such service usually entails downward mobility and an identification with the poor whom Jesus calls blessed. While such an identification may not win us the accolades of this world, it does bring us closer to the fellowship of the Suffering Servant.

MEDITATION: *When our future is in the hands of Christ, it is in the safe-keeping of the one who will gently lead us forward.*

The coming kingdom

'The closer this kingdom is and the more its coming
is God's doing, the more must human beings conform to it by a radical change in their way of life.'

Jon Sobrino

While we may act as signposts of the kingdom
of God and at best embody in our life together
and in our service to the world something of the
presence of the kingdom, the kingdom is wholly
God's doing. And because it is God's action
amongst us, it calls for continual change on our
part. For on the way to worship, God may call us
instead to serve our neighbour. In building our
structures for doing social good, God may instead call us to walk the way of prayer. And in
the midst of thinking that we have done so well,
God may challenge us about our pride and self-
sufficiency. God's kingdom is always an irruption,
since it ruffles the smooth flow of tradition and
calls the new into being.

THOUGHT: *While God's kingly reign is evident in
the world, it should be most clearly revealed in the
lives of those who acknowledge his Lordship.*

The power of love

'For not only do people need food, but they need also the touch of a hand, the sound of a voice. For food lasts but a day, but Love is for always'.

Mother Teresa

In the midst of grappling with finding the most appropriate strategies for helping the poor, we must not forget the power of love. All the strategies of self-help, group mobilisation and empowerment will be skewed if love is absent. Moreover, there will always be those in our society for whom strategies of self-help are inappropriate. The sick and dying and those with severe intellectual disabilities need care rather than self-help. And we will also come across those in society who have been so 'wounded' that they first need loving care and healing before they can once again begin to assume responsibility for their own lives. The important lesson in all of this is that we never lose sight of the individual in the midst of our caring and helping strategies.

PRAYER: *Lord, grant me the power to love and to serve those whom I judge to be unlovable.* Amen.

God in history

'God's self-revelation occurs in the context of a history of conflict; it is also clear that in this history God is on the side of the subjugated.'

Elsa Tamez

God does not stand on the sideline of history idly watching our attempts at empire building or our vain struggles to achieve greater power and control. The idea of a God detached from human affairs is not the biblical picture of God. Neither is the idea that God enters the fray at our bidding. God is hardly a proponent of our right-wing or left-wing politics. God has his own agenda and concerns. These concerns have to do with justice, mercy and salvation rather than with our particular causes. While God is concerned about the maintenance of the fabric and good order of society, the God of justice is particularly concerned to bring liberation to the oppressed.

THOUGHT: *By making us and giving us a place to be, God is the God of history. The good news is that God has also fully entered our history in the person of the Son.*

Setting captives free

'When we are not breaking the yoke of oppression,
we have no good news for the poor.'

Vishal Mangalwadi

Good news for the poor is not simply that God
loves them. In the past, this message has been
used to keep the poor in their state of misery. In
fact, poverty was glorified as a reality especially
pleasing to God. Instead, good news for the poor
is that God is the liberator and that we as his people
have been enlisted in the cause of setting captives
free. This activity is not simply political activity.
The poor do need justice. They do need friends
who will argue their case. The poor do need
economic help. They need those who will share
generously with them. But they also need a new
self and to be empowered with new hope. This can
come through the realisation that God is working
on their behalf.

THOUGHT: *God chooses to work through his people.
God is prepared, however, to use anyone as an instrument of transformation.*

God's challenge

'They do not want a God who will question us and trouble our consciences, a God who cries out; "Cain! What have you done to your brother Abel?"'

Rutilio Grande

While God is the one who brings comfort and blessing, God is also the one who calls us to account. In love, God confronts us and, because our Redeemer is merciful, he disciplines us. Likewise, after having responded themselves to God's call for justice, God's servants need to challenge others. These others are not only the faithful in the Christian community, but also the rulers in the land. No-one is exempt from God's call. Rulers are to be God's servants of righteousness and are never to be a law unto themselves. When they do begin to live only for themselves, they will incur God's hand of correction. But they can also find God's heart of mercy.

MEDITATION: *While God's challenge involves a painful exposure, its purpose is to bring forth justice and peace.*

A people's church

'The church for which we yearned, the community of liberty and love, was not found in the confines of the ecclesial organisation.'

Rubem Alves

Church is people in relationship under the Lordship of Christ. It is primarily not about institutional and organisational realities. But since these realities so easily become the primary focus, the church must be constantly deinstitutionalised. Church must be structured for community, solidarity, sharing life together and walking the common road. It has to do with friendship and sharing the common joys and difficulties of life. It is a community free from manipulation and control. It is a fellowship of worship, prayer and listening to scripture and one that has its arms open to the world. It is, therefore, a servant community that has by no means arrived, but knows how to celebrate along the way.

PRAYER: *Lord, you so much want your people to be a people of hope and joy, but also a people of generosity and servanthood. Grant that we may not lose our way by playing church instead of seeking to participate in your kingdom. Amen.*

Turning it for good

'Our blackness. . . is not a lamentable fact because. . . it affords us the glorious privilege and opportunity to further the gospel of love, forgiveness and reconciliation.'

Desmond Tutu

Our world is full of prejudice. Bias and intolerance lurk in all of our hearts. Yet, what we may despise God will exalt. What we reject God welcomes and what we may regard as nothing God uses for his glory. God has a wonderful way of turning the tables. Those who are self-sufficient need to learn from others and those who have been rejected can demonstrate the power of forgiveness and reconciliation. Thus weakness becomes a strength and suffering becomes the road to being peacemakers. This is the politics of reversal. This is the wisdom of the upside down kingdom of God. This is what confounds the world and calls an indolent church to repentance. This is the way that catches us all by surprise.

THOUGHT: *God will always side with 'the little ones' of the earth who turn Godward in faith and hope.*

The God in front of us

'God is pro-vocative — he calls us forward, and is only to be found as one who goes forward with his people in a constant process of uprooting.'

Hugo Assmann

Moving forward implies leaving things behind. This is never easy. We frequently prefer the familiar even when it causes us difficulty or distress. Moreover, we become so used to what we experience that we can hardly believe that a better way is possible. It is at this point that God demonstrates that he has our interests at heart. For God knows what is possible — and God can see what lies ahead. The Almighty knows what is best for us. So he comes to disturb us and to call us forward. The challenge for us is to believe God more than our present circumstances. It is believing that what God alone can see at this point in time, we will one day experience.

MEDITATION: *Being called forward is finally a matter of faith and obedience. It is never a matter of ironclad guarantees.*

Obedience

'Obedience is not a consequence of our knowledge of God, just as it is not a precondition for it: obedience is our knowledge of God.'

José Míguez Bonino

We tend to emphasise that we know something first and our obedience comes next. Obedience is a response to what we know. In fact, we make the point: how can you obey if you don't know? While there is a lot of truth in this observation, it is not the whole story. Things also work the other way round. In our obedience we also come to understand more fully what God is asking of us. Often the first steps of our obedience aren't all that crystal clear. We have a 'sense' of what we are to do, but specifics are usually lacking. Consequently, obedience will always be a walk of faith. And those who never begin to walk the way of obedience will never really know all that much.

MEDITATION: *Obedience is the essence of truth.*

The power of community

'But no human force can crush a coherent community, for it is a living God who dwells there and listens to the outcry of his people'.

Dom Helder Camara

Community is not a human achievement. It is God's creation and gift. Thus, the essence of community is not organisation, but relationships forged by a common dependence on the God who is building a new humanity. Therefore, the power of community lies not in a particular mode of being together. It springs from the presence of the living God who abides with those who seek him and expect to find there life's sustenance and direction from the God of all grace. Community, therefore, should not be governed by ideology or structures. These will only become constricting and oppressive. Instead, it should be ruled by the Prince of Peace and the Father of Consolation. Such a community will not only experience purpose and direction, but also true freedom.

THOUGHT: *Those who stand together will not easily fall.*

Radical change

'The enemy. . . has been less the atheist than the in-
human.'

Jon Sobrino

The major challenge in the Third World is not
the discovery of the God of meaning, but finding
the God of liberation. It is not so much a matter
of finding life's purpose as it is the struggle for
survival. It is not the challenge to live a simple
lifestyle, but to stave off the spectre of hunger
and despair. Christians in the Third World, as a
consequence, face very different issues. This has
given birth to a theology all of their own. But
liberation theology also has relevance for the
First World. There also we find the poor, the
marginalised and the neglected who experience
inhumanity and oppression. These also do not
need an intellectualised theology and a guilt-
motivated charity. They need companionship
and empowerment, grace and dignity, and hope
and opportunity.

MEDITATION: *God's passion for justice calls men
and women to work for a new world.*

Incarnational spirituality

'Spirituality must be incarnated and. . . the privileged place of faith's incarnation is in one's relationship to one's brother or sister.'

Segundo Galilea

No greater criticism can be levelled at the church than its failure to care for its own, particularly those who are different, struggling, weak and impoverished. Since charity must begin at home, the practice of love and care in the Christian community is the training ground for the church's wider role in society. The call to do good to those in the household of faith is not an invitation to become inwardly focussed. Instead, it is the basis for providing credibility for everything else that we seek to do in society. The church itself is to become the model of the change which it is seeking to bring to society. It should demonstrate in its common life the hope that a new way is possible.

THOUGHT: *Servanthood should not be the preoccupation of the few, but the lifestyle of the many.*

Servanthood

'Equality within the community was the equality that all were to be servants.'

Vinay Samuel

There will always be differences in the Christian community. Some are more prosperous than others. Some are more articulate. Some have outstanding gifts. Some seem to be more hopeful, while others struggle with doubts and fears. There is nothing uniform about such a community. It is as diverse as life itself. Yet it must find a commonality if it is to be a community. Such a commonality is not only to be found in an acknowledgment of Christ's significance for the community, but also in finding practical ways to serve each other. While we will never all be the same, a common desire to support and encourage each other binds people together in the gentle rhythm of giving and receiving.

PRAYER: *Lord, give me a heart that is big enough to look to the needs of others.*   Amen.

Joining the poor

'The evangelically poor will establish solidarity
with the economically poor.'
                                                    Leonardo and Clodovis Boff

It is one thing to preach and to provide help. It is
quite another to join with those in need and make a
common journey with them. It is always much easier
to give something. It is harder to give ourselves. Just
as it is much easier to advise than to listen, so we
readily give but maintain our distance. Yet the poor
need friendship more than help and companionship
more than aid. They invite us to feel their pain and
participate in their hope. They want us to share in
the little they have rather than be the objects of our
pity. Thus, those who wish to be poor for the sake of
the gospel and who wish to join with the economically
poor must come as partners and not as providers.
They must come to learn and to receive; not simply to
give.

THOUGHT: *Being poor for the sake of the gospel does not
mean that we will be completely like those who are economically poor. But we will be able to learn from them.*

Fundamentalism

'The fundamentalist solution frees us from our painful encounter with a reality that ever remains incomplete, changing, upsetting and distressing.'

Rubem Alves

Fundamentalist Christianity attempts to make the complexity of life simple. It attempts to make life controllable and explainable. It majors on slick explanations. It has answers for everything, although it fails to recognise that these answers usually hold good only for a very narrow slice of reality. The difficulty with this approach to life is not only that it fails to identify the struggle and questioning that takes place in scripture, but it fails to understand the nature of faith. For faith has its certainties and its questions. Faith has its consolations, but also its pain. Faith has its accomplishments as well as its defeats. Faith knows what it believes, but also reaches out for further answers.

MEDITATION: *A faith that cannot face all of life is a faith that is insecure and immature.*

February

. . .our journey will always be one of faith rather than certainty.

Forging the new

'Traveller, there is no path: you make paths by walking.'

Hugo Assmann

While it is true that we have the example of scripture to guide our footsteps, each of us must nevertheless make his or her own journey. Much of it will come as a surprise, for life is not that predictable and much is outside of our control. Thus, our journey will always be one of faith rather than certainty. The challenge is to forge ahead knowing that God has gone before us in the footprints of the Suffering Servant. The further challenge is to take ample time to reflect on what that journey is all about so that we may learn its wisdom.

THOUGHT: *Those who wait for final certainty will never make the journey. Those who plunge ahead and never evaluate will learn little along the way. Those who act in faith and prayerfully reflect will see the hand of God.*

The covenant

'It is a covenant that is as broad as possible in scope, as noble and beautiful as anything that has ever been devised, forceful and replete with rewards and punishments.'

Carmen Guerrero Nakpil

God's commandments provide a framework by which we can order our lives. They are not based on God's demand, but on grace. They are not the means by which we gain God's favour, but the means by which we express our gratitude. The commandments show us how to respond to God and how to serve our neighbour. They provide a morality that can become the ethos of every nation. However, the primary challenge is that they become the values by which I order my life. While it is one thing that I do not steal from my neighbour, it is quite another that I do not covet what my neighbour possesses. The latter speaks of matters of the heart. And it is there where the battle for personal morality is won or lost.

PRAYER: *Lord, give me a heart that truly loves to do your will even when that may be difficult and challenging.* Amen.

A matter of perspective

'Our perspective on reality changes according to the standpoint from which we examine it.'

Ruben Alves

We see the same reality differently. Some saw Jesus as only a prophet. Others were convinced that he was a troublemaker. Some believed that he was the messiah. What we see is always subject to interpretation — and we frequently interpret things differently depending on our social location. While the poor heard Jesus gladly, the religious leaders were suspicious of Jesus lest he threaten their power over the people. Similarly, those presently in power are likely to see things differently than those who are marginalised. And the rich will always find a way to justify their perspectives on life. But the rich and the poor can find common ground in a commitment to kingdom values.

MEDITATION: *Those who undergo a change of location usually undergo a change of perspective.*

Against oppressors

'God sides with the oppressed against the pharaohs of this world.'

Leonardo and Clodovis Boff

God also cares about the pharaohs of this world, but requires that they repent and do his bidding. Unlike us, God is not impressed with the station of the rich or the powerful. God does not measure people by their social position, but looks for the heart that loves to do his will and is not self-seeking. The Great Liberator looks for those who will join him in his passion for justice. Thus, the powerful will have to make difficult choices for, in embracing God's concerns, they will have to make choices against themselves. This is the nature of true repentance. True faith acknowledges that God knows best and his judgment is right. Because the powerful so seldom acknowledge that God has the final word, they work against rather than for the new world that God is shaping.

THOUGHT: *The problem is not that the powerful are powerful. It is that they refuse to become servants of God.*

In the world

'Most individual Christians tend to understand their relationship with God in total isolation from their social context.'

Vinay Samuel

Our love for God should draw us into the arena of life, for God's concern is not simply for the church, but also the world. It is not only faith that sustains us, but also the good order of the earth. Life is not only lived spiritually, but also naturally. Thus, we celebrate God as both redeemer and creator. God is the one who gives us meaning and direction, but also sustains us through the world he has made. Therefore, just as we are to give God due praise for his grace and mercy, we are also to give him thanks by caring for the earth and by working for justice in our society. We cannot be unconcerned about natural things, for these are God's handiwork. These also manifest the glory of God.

THOUGHT: *Every Christian should be 'worldly' and spiritual at the same time.*

Following Jesus

'It is the real following of Jesus that enables one to
understand the reality of Jesus.'

Jon Sobrino

Nothing undermines discipleship more than the idea
that Christ has suffered on our behalf and we merely
have to receive his benefits. While it is true that Christ
carried the guilt and shame that was only ours, it is
not true that we are simply beneficiaries. Christ's
death on our behalf involves us in a death of our
own — death to our old ways of being and acting.
What Christ has done for us involves us existential-
ly. He was obedient where we were unfaithful; but
he calls us to a similar obedience. He brought glory
to the Father while we are so persistently self-seeking;
but he calls us to seek first God's way and his
kingdom. Faith in Christ binds us to become like
him. Consequently, we will have to walk a similar
road in our concrete jungles, even though we are
far away from the dusty by-ways of Galilee.

PRAYER: *Lord, since faith involves my obedience,
help me to be faithful to you because of your great love
for me.* Amen.

Spiritual intimacy

'[God] wishes not only to give man being and life, but also to draw him into the very intimacy of his own life.'
Dom Helder Camara

We experience God in many ways. Sometimes, God is powerful and overwhelming; at other times, stern and correcting. But God is also loving and nurturing. God is the strong One to whom we go for protection, but is also the One who heals and nourishes us, thereby empowering us for life's journey. We may experience God not only in the midst of our daily work or in specific acts of Christian service, but also in times of quietude and reflection. God is as welcoming when we pray, worship and meditate on his works and words as he is pleased when we actively serve him in the church and in the world. Sadly, some Christians are so bent on being active that they fail to experience God's goodness even when they are still and reflective.

PRAYER: *Lord, thank you that you sustain me in my life of work and service. Thank you, also, that you welcome me to rest in your love and presence so that I may find fuel for the journey of life.* Amen.

Commitment to pray

'Prayer is not easy or spontaneous; it requires a renewed choice each day.'

Segundo Galilea

There is nothing easy about prayer, for it is not as natural as breathing. Prayer more frequently arises out of a situation of difficulty or need. When life takes on an easy rhythm, because all is well, then prayer often ebbs away. In order for prayer to become more central, it is necessary for it to be beyond mere circumstance. Its central impulse should not be whether things are difficult or going well. Instead, prayer should be a commitment to relationship building. It is a response to the God who so amazingly invites us into the kingdom. It is a response to the God who journeys with us and sustains us along the way. It is being mesmerised by the God of all grace who pours love upon us. If prayer is not concerned with a relationship in response to God's love, it will hardly survive on the rack of formalism or the vicissitudes of life.

MEDITATION: *A renewed response to the God who incessantly invites us into fellowship is the best response we can make.*

In Jesus' name

'Be Jesus to everyone you meet and, in everyone you meet, see Jesus.'

Mother Teresa

Those of us from the Western world are much more likely to want to be Jesus to others; and we are much less likely to be able to see Jesus in others. This is because we assume that we have so much to give and that those to whom we minister lack so much. This is sheer arrogance on our part. So much of our life is still broken and we are at best wounded healers. If, however, we come to others with greater humility, recognising that Jesus has already gone before us and that he has already touched the other with the marks of his grace, then a much more holistic approach is possible. Then the focus shifts from what we have to give to what Christ will do in the situation. Then there is the possibility that the Christ in me will join the Christ who has gone before me.

MEDITATION: *To be Jesus to others means that I must become more Christlike myself.*

Prophetic compassion

'There is no dearth of Christian service today. But because much of it is service without prophetic compassion, it is powerless to bring about a radical change in individuals and society.'

Vishal Mangalwadi

The word 'compassion' has a nice warm feel to it. Prophetic compassion sounds much more ominous — but it carries a much greater promise. For while compassion so frequently connotes the gift of comfort in the midst of difficulty, prophetic compassion is concerned with radical change. This kind of compassion, while not without the ability to bring comfort, is concerned about injustice and the forces of oppression. It loves to the point of action. It cares to the point of protest. It speaks in the midst of involvement. It prays in the valley of pain. And it fearlessly speaks the word of truth to oppressors at the cost of one's own safety. Such compassion arises from an encounter with the man from Galilee who takes us onto the dusty roads of this world.

THOUGHT: *True servanthood is always concerned with liberation.*

The impulse to life

'Of all the lessons that they [the poor] taught me. . .
the most important was to shun death and embrace
life.'

Jean-Bertrand Aristide

The poor live in death-dealing circumstances.
They are both the victims of oppression and of
an inner fatalism. The pernicious cycle of lack of
education, employment, health and opportunity
condemns them to eke out a meagre existence.
But there are also powerful life forces in the
slums of despair — the crowded alleys with
children at play; the resolute women working
several back-breaking jobs; the men in faraway
lands as contract workers. All these are fuelled
by a powerful hope that the future and not the
present has the last word. Anyone who has been
with the poor cannot but marvel at the fact that
God is somehow there edging them forward,
stemming the tide of despair and empowering
them with resoluteness.

THOUGHT: *The poor most often evangelise those
who have come to help them.*

The following of Jesus

'Individualism and spiritualism. . . combine to impoverish and even distort the following of Jesus.'

Gustavo Gutiérrez

While we are individually called to follow Jesus, our discipleship is not an individual affair. Jesus calls disciples into community where we serve one another, encourage each other and become accountable to our brothers and sisters in Christ. In solidarity, this community is called not to face inward, but outward. It exists to serve the world. It is there as an agent of transformation. It is a signpost to the coming kingdom of God. Neither individualism nor piety are key in the following of Jesus. Instead, solidarity and costly service more closely characterise a life of discipleship. If following Jesus is simply for ourselves, we distort the purpose of the Suffering Servant.

MEDITATION: *Our discipleship begins in the embrace of Jesus. It is furthered in the embrace of the community of faith. It comes to fruition in service to the world.*

The prophetic word

'The prophetic word is still valid for us and for our time.'
Dom Helder Camara

A prophetic word can be a word of encouragement, correction or direction spoken to the community of believers. But a prophetic word can
also be addressed to the world. This needs to be
an embodied word; it needs to be a word that expresses what the community of faith is modelling. While the church has a responsibility to call
into question the powers of our age, it must resist
cheap sloganeering. The church can hardly point
the finger while its own practice is in disarray.
The prophetic word, therefore, must first bring
the church to wholehearted conversion before it
can become a word addressed to the world. This
is not to suggest that the church must first be perfect. But it does imply that the prophetic word is
all the more powerful when it is first lived.

PRAYER: *Lord, as we are transformed may we be
empowered to challenge others.* Amen.

Adult roles

'From a fundamentally passive role within church structures, women are moving toward adult responsibility for the church's life and worship.'

Katherine Gilfeather

Women have always played a key role in the life of the church. But they have frequently been relegated to peripheral responsibilites. This has changed significantly in recent years. Among the churches of the poor, many women provide leadership and pastoral care. And in community organising and in community development, the contribution of women has been outstanding. The liberation of women and the resultant equal partnership with men has produced a richer quality of service and a more genuine modelling of Christian community. For God has created and redeemed both women and men to reflect his image and has charged both with leadership and responsibility to shape the world and to build communities of faith.

REFLECTION: *Partnership, rather than competition, will build a better world.*

For Christ

'Service in solidarity with the oppressed also implies an act of love for the suffering Christ.'

Leonardo and Clodovis Boff

Christian work with marginalised people is
never simply doing social work or community
development. Instead, it is the work of building
the human community, as well as building the
community of believers, in the name of Christ. It
is doing community work motivated by the compassion of Christ. It is serving people for the sake
of Christ. And because every person bears the
mark of God and is a potential brother or sister in
Christ, it is serving the hidden Christ in others.
None of this means that we serve simply with
the other's conversion in view. We serve
anyway, whether people come to faith in Christ,
or not. We rejoice when some do, and faithfully
continue to serve those who don't.

THOUGHT: *To serve the hidden Christ in others may
well cause them to embrace the revealed Christ.*

Holistic values

'Not to kill includes paying a living wage to the workers.'

Carmen Guerrero Nakpil

In a sea of corruption, it is easy to trumpet a singular virtue. A Christian business person may proudly assert, 'But I provide employment for many people from among the urban poor and encourage staff Bible studies and, as a result, many have come to faith in Christ.' While no one should negate this business person's contribution, there are other issues that also require attention if we are to express holistic values. And one issue is the payment of just wages. Not only do many employers in the Third world, including Christians, fail to pay the basic wage, but that wage is well below minimal living standards. In thinking holistically, we need to join body and soul, the material and the spiritual, the secular and the sacred, and evangelism and justice.

REFLECTION: *In the dialectic of work and worker, the benefit to the worker must be the higher value. This does not negate the need for profitability or the value of the work.*

Non-persons

'The worst crime that can be laid at the door of the white person. . . is not our economic, social and political exploitation. . . It is that the white's policy succeeded in filling most of us with a self-disgust and self-hatred.'

Desmond Tutu

Colonialism was a collusion of trader and missionary, of gun and word, of exploitation and Christianisation. But in our post-colonial world, this mixed legacy has left its festering sores. Some of these are visible. Third World poverty continues to dehumanise millions of people. Other sores are less visible. Fractured cultures, ambivalent values and confused identities are its tragic manifestations. This calls for a greater global justice, but also for a theology that affirms the good in culture and a church practice that allows people to express their national uniqueness in the worship of God.

THOUGHT: *Can the demons of the colonial legacy be exorcised and can national, cultural and individual healing occur both through prayer and social reconstruction?*

Loving deeds

'The important thing is not how much we accomplish, but how much love we put into our deeds every day.'

Mother Teresa

Compulsive and frenetic activity won't necessarily win the day — much doing doesn't of itself accomplish much. Our activity needs to be focussed. It needs to be discerning. It particularly needs to be empowering lest it merely evokes gratitude, but breeds dependency. Therefore, the critical question is not simply what we do, but how we do it. While the how has to do with strategies, it also has to do with motivation. And deeds done in joyful love rather than an exacting legalism or unresolved guilt carry with them a window into the loving heart of God. Deeds should always be signposts pointing to the gentler world desired by the God of all grace and compassion. If this is to occur, then deeds must be bathed in God's love.

PRAYER: *Lord, fill my heart and my deeds with your love.* Amen.

Justice

'My faith, as it grew and deepened, made me more sensitive to injustice.'

Caesar Molebatsi

Some people, when they become Christians, become dogmatic and rigid in their thinking. Others throw their mind away and become anti-intellectual. But others become other-worldly. They turn their face away from the world towards the sanctuary. The opposite should, in fact, occur. Our growing love for Christ, the deepening of our walk of faith and our commitment to discipleship call us to face the world with all its concerns and injustices. Christians should be known not only for their commitment to the truth of scripture and for their personal piety, but also for their passion for justice. Christians should be as concerned for human rights issues as for evangelism; for personal growth as for social transformation; for the development of an interior spirituality as for a spirituality that embraces the issues of our time.

MEDITATION: *The passion of justice must be driven not by hatred, but by the love of Christ.*

Agent of transformation

'The church is to confront the world and to seek to be an agent of change. . . when the church does not confront the world. . . it is conforming to the world.'
Vinay Samuel

The church has many tasks in the world. This does not mean that the church does not also exist for the glory of God and for the well-being of its members. But the church has a multiple role in the world. Key is to proclaim good news and to disciple men and women in following Christ. The church may also create institutions of education and care and is called to preserve all that is good in society. But the church also has more radical responsibilites. It must call into question the idolatrous powers of this age. It must work for justice as well as for reconciliation. It should be a prophetic voice. It can only do these things, however, when it is not aligned with the power brokers and the ideologies of this age, but lives solely for the kingdom of God.

REFLECTION: *The power of the church as an agent of transformation lies in its conformity to Christ's proclamation of the kingdom of God.*

Work of hope

'My work has always been to support the hope of my people. If there is even a spark of hope, it is my duty to nourish it.'

Oscar Romero

While most of us wish that we could provide lasting solutions for the poor, the marginalised and the needy, answers are usually not so readily available. The poor are often the victims of oppression. The marginalised are frequently victimised. And the needy may have a range of difficulties for which there are no easy answers. But there are ways in which we can be of help. We can walk the road with the poor and needy. We can be in solidarity with them. We can make their issues our cause. We can make their burdens our concern. We can identify with their struggles and advocate on their behalf. This form of identification will not only bless them; it will also bless the giver. In serving the poor, our own life is sustained by the Christ who accompanies us.

PRAYER: *Lord, in the midst of so much pain and suffering, help me not to stand idly by or to become bitter, but give me the gift of solidarity.* Amen.

Historical practice

'The basic characteristic of faith is its historical practice.'
                                                Hugo Assmann

Faith looks back to the cross of Christ and embraces its redemptive power. And faith joyfully looks to the future when God's final kingdom will be established. But faith also faces the contemporary world. Faith in Christ is manifested in obedience. And obedience involves walking the Christ-road. This road has to do with preaching good news. But it also involves confronting the powers of this age. Jesus healed the sick. He also threw the money changers out of the temple. And equally importantly, he embraced the poor and founded an alternative community which functioned in the midst of life. The walk of faith is not simply internal piety. It is a way of life that is concerned with our neighbour and advocates justice in our broken world. If faith has no direct bearing on the pain of our world, it is not Christian faith.

THOUGHT: *Faith embraces the world in order to transform it.*

Prophetic witness

'Jesus and his new community were naturally and intentionally a threat to the establishment.'

Vishal Mangalwadi

Jesus has been called the fifth option man. He did not join the ruling elite, the Sadducees; or the religious zealous, the Pharisees; or the political radicals, the Zealots; or the world-denying communitarians, the Essenes. Jesus and his disciples walked a different road marked by love for the Father; a passion for the kingdom of God; the practice of reconciliation; and a commitment to the poor. They were the misfits. They had a different vision of life and they lived a different lifestyle. More particularly, no power block in Israel could coopt or control them. Thus they were a threat to the powers of their day.

REFLECTION: *So often the church is in collusion with the elite or with the values of contemporary society. This only shows how much the church still needs to be converted.*

The whole of life

'A spirituality is not restricted to the so-called religious aspect of life. . . because the whole of human life, personal and communal, is involved in the journey.'

Gustavo Gutiérrez

Spirituality has both a vertical and horizontal dimension. It has to do with love for God and love of neighbour. It involves prayer, meditation and reflection and proclamation and witness. It brings together the journey of faith and that of practical service. While spirituality has a lot to do with the individual's devotional life, it has everything to do with communal reality as well. For spirituality is both nurtured and sustained within the community of faith and finds practical expression in the general community.

REFLECTION: *One's relationship with God is both intensely personal and communal. Therefore spirituality can be both ecstatic and practical.*

Solidarity

'The light of solidarity is the one beacon that we the oppressed have to light our way through the dark corners and byways of our little world.'

Jean-Bertrand Aristide

The poor in the Third World are the victims of structural injustice. The little that they earn from a long day of labour is only enough to put food on the table. Nothing is left for anything else. This sad reality is often overlaid with alcohol abuse, fatalism and loss of hope. Therefore, the communities of the poor need to be empowered. This empowerment can come not only from a new-found faith in Christ, but also from building a community of faith where pain is shared and people stand in solidarity. Such a community, from the underside of history, provides not only prayer support and encouragement, but also builds cooperatives and other joint ventures. When the poor in their vulnerability stand shoulder to shoulder, then strength can come to do that which on their own would overwhelm them.

PRAYER: *Lord, whatever we may do for the poor or give to them, may we above all help them to find the gift of true community.* Amen.

The goods of the earth

'The goods of the earth which should have served to unite us, to foster cooperation, are the occasion of discord and division.'

Arturo Paoli

While spirituality has everything to do with one's relationship to God, it also embraces the practical realities of life. Love for God does not allow me to hate my neighbour. And love for my neighbour involves practical care and sharing. While so much of the world's agenda is competitive resulting in the strong becoming richer, the ethos of the Christian community is cooperation. For that community, the question is: How can I use what God has bountifully given me to serve my brothers and sisters in Christ and my neighbour who may yet become a fellow traveller in the faith? In this kind of sharing, we truly break bread together.

MEDITATION: *The resources of the earth are sufficient for our need, not for our greed. Greed robs our neighbour and produces alienation. Sharing, on the other hand, blesses our neighbour and builds community.*

Revealing

'Every worker becomes known through his creation. And when he created light and the stars, the heaven and the earth, God was expressing himself, he was communicating.'

Antidio, a campesino

Something of the nature of God is expressed in the natural world, but who God is is more fully expressed in the coming of Jesus. And what Jesus said and did gives us a window into the beauty of God's kingdom. This kingdom overcomes enmity with reconciliation. Power is expressed in servanthood. Legalism is replaced by grace. Good news is for the poor. Healing is for those who acknowledge their need. Touched by the mystery of this kingdom, our own lives can become a window to the heart of God. Thus, we become known by what we do, not simply by what we believe. In our doing, our being is revealed. And when our being is graced by the love of God, our doing will also reveal something of the Great Lover.

REFLECTION: *The gentle movement of God is always from invisibility to revelation. Thus, faith is not based on mystery, but on word and deed.*

Kingdom in history

'The coming of the kingdom. . . the coming of God's rule, is always interwoven with what is human and what is ordinary.'

Melba Maggay

God has come amongst us in the person of Jesus, and his kingdom is revealed wherever the work of Jesus is continued. That work is not only men and women coming to new-found faith, or experiencing forgiveness or healing, but also when peace and justice spring into being in our distorted world. Many times, the work of Jesus is continued by the church. But sometimes the work of Jesus is done outside the church by men and women of goodwill, by those who work for peace and justice in situations of oppression. This is not to suggest that this work is a complete manifestation of the kingdom, since the kingdom involves God's rule over all of our lives; but it is a part of the work of kingdom in which the church needs to play a more active role.

THOUGHT: *Work for the kingdom is cooperation with God to achieve all that is good for our world.*

March

Jesus welcomes all:
not in order to pity,
but to renew.

Hope in despair

'We have all known persons who have lost every-thing and have not lost the joy of living; persons who are imprisoned unjustly and do not lose their peace and tranquillity; persons who live in misery and take in orphans; persons who have suffered injustices and seek to reestablish justice with no desire to revenge.'

Segundo Galilea

Struggle and difficulty do not necessarily end in hopelessness and despair. The opposite may, in fact, occur. Difficulty may produce sensitivity, care and generosity. This mirrors something of the mystery of life when the opposite of what is normally expected occurs. This is not only the mystery of life, but also the mystery of the kingdom of God. In the kingdom of God, amazing reversals occur. The poor are blessed and the rich remain empty-handed. The good guy is the ethnic outsider — the Samaritan; and the bad guys are those of the religious estab-lishment. A sign that God is at work in our tragic world is when evil is expected, but good emerges.

THOUGHT: *If God does reversals, on which side are you now?*

The compassionate Christ

'If you look at the cross, you will see his head lowered to kiss you.'
                                        Mother Teresa

In Jesus, God has drawn near with outstretched arms. With him is the welcome to come as you are. Confused. Fearful. Hurting. Doubting. Struggling. Young and full of life. Poor and dying. Successful and influential. Marginalised and bitter. Competent and dynamic. The welcome is for all. For all need the embrace of acceptance — the striving business person as much as the wayward teenager; or the poor, broken by the hardships of life, need to be loved for who they are in their success or difficulty. Jesus welcomes all — not in order to pity, but to renew. His embrace is more than one of understanding and compassion. His touch changes us. He does not simply pat us on the shoulder. He gently renews us in the very depths of our being. There, where we are unknown and uncared for, he enters to make us new.

PRAYER: *Lord Jesus, I need to see your eyes upon me and your hands outstretched in welcome, for I need to come to you much more than I care to admit.* Amen.

To begin again

'The important thing is to begin again, humbly and courageously, after every fall.'

Dom Helder Camara

A fatal stubbornness seems to pervade our lives. We find it so hard to admit that we are wrong or have wronged others. And so we defend our rationalisations and our actions. Sometimes, we even find it difficult to acknowledge that our project has failed and that our work and struggle seemingly has been in vain. These forms of denial push us away from the wellsprings of life. The power of life does not lie in our successes. These are soon tarnished and fade away. Instead, the source of life lies in our willingness to acknowledge our emptiness or our fault so that we can be renewed by the God of all grace. The community of faith, therefore, consists not of those who have arrived, but of those who continue to seek sustenance in the long journey.

MEDITATION: *When everything has fallen away, we become candidates for the greater riches because our hands are empty.*

Misunderstood

'Men and women who try to side with the dispossessed and bear witness to God in Latin America must accept the bitter fact that they will inevitably be suspect.'

Gustavo Gutiérrez

Following Christ is often a bitter-sweet experience, for doing what he asks of us doesn't always lead to success or happiness. In walking the costly road of discipleship, we don't always see the fruit that we expect. And we certainly will not always be kindly thought of by our peers. In engaging in a ministry to the outcasts of society, we ourselves may well experience rejection. This will certainly occur when, through our solidarity with the poor, we call for change. And if that call for change involves a change of values as well as of the system, we can easily be regarded as troublemakers or traitors.

REFLECTION: *Jesus was regarded as a trouble-maker in Israel. For this he was crucified. Those who truly follow his example will come into conflict with the powers that be.*

Resistance

'Christians have not been brought up to fight.
They've been brought up to accept their lot, to conform.'

Arturo Paoli

This is true of many Christians. They are conservative and don't want to rock the boat. Others
take a passive approach to life. Things will always be bad, they say, so why make life difficult
by trying to change things? Others are so
heavenly minded that they are no earthly good.
They are on earth waiting for heaven and fail to
see that they have any responsibility for what is
happening here. But there are Christians who
don't fall into these broad categorisations. Shaped
by the example of Jesus, they have a radical and
proactive approach to life. They believe that they
have a responsibility for this world and see
themselves as change agents.

THOUGHT: *Jesus the man of peace was also the man
of resistance. We are called to follow his example.*

Face to face

'In making the Father known. . . Jesus seems to have engaged himself less in addressing large crowds than in the more exhausting and costly tasks of meeting people face to face with their sickness and sins and fears.'

Melba Maggay

The call of Jesus first of all invites us to face our own sins, fears and need before challenging us to care for our brothers and sisters in Christ, our family or our neighbour. Having experienced something of the liberation and renewal of Christ in our lives, we can become the hands of healing for others. In this ministry, we are challenged to draw near to the other in order to listen, identify and enter the places of pain. Having bent our ears and our heart to the one in need, we may then reach out hands of healing and care.

REFLECTION: *Effective ministry joins head, heart and hands.*

Leadership

'Transforming leaders are empowered individuals who seek to empower a given people.'

Joel Ortiz

Leaders not only empower people, but people also empower leaders. Archbishop Oscar Romero became a fearless Christian leader in turbulent El Salvador. The faithful suffering of his priests and his people inspired him to greater faithfulness and boldness. The movement of empowerment, therefore, is never one way — from leader to people. Even though the leader has great responsibility to focus, train, mobilise, encourage, correct and evaluate the people with whom he or she is working, the leader also receives. This synergistic relationship means that the whole is more than the sum of the parts. Leader and people working together in unity can accomplish much for the kingdom of God.

THOUGHT: *Leaders are often only as good as the people who will work with them.*

Christ and the church

'Christ founded the church so that he himself could go on being present in the history of humanity.'

Oscar Romero

Jesus Christ is the risen Lord. He is also present in the church when the community of faith obediently responds to the good news of the gospel and to the work of the Holy Spirit. This does not mean that the church fully represents Christ, because the church itself needs to grow into the fullness and likeness of Christ. But Jesus wishes to work through the church. It is to be his voice. It is to be his healing hands outstretched to the world. The church is, therefore, involved in a joyful and awesome task. Joyful, because the community of faith lives out of the grace and love of Christ. Awesome, because the people of God are to continue in our contemporary world the very works that Christ did when on earth.

MEDITATION: *The works of Christ involve recon-ciliation and peacemaking, and the work of mercy and justice. How can our fumbling hands carry such treasures to a hurting humanity?*

For others

'Ultimately, God saves the oppressed for the sake of
their oppressors.'

Desmond Tutu

God seems to have a strange way of working in
history. While being committed to the salvation
and transformation of all, God frequently picks
unlikely candidates to be the bearers of his good
news. God seems to work in the underside of
history and frequently renewal and revival
movements have impacted the poor and marginalised. Yet these blessings are never for them
alone. If the poor can proclaim good news to
those who have exploited them, then great is
their salvation and powerful is their witness.
When those who have good reason to show bitterness show kindness instead, then the power of
the gospel is unleashed.

PRAYER: *Lord, help me to be part of your great purpose to bring good news to all. Help me particularly to
be a bearer of your forgiveness to others.* Amen.

Things of concern

'The deeper our communion, the greater the freedom to bring to God anything and everything of concern to us.'

Isabelo Magalit

We often carry far more than we are able. As a result, the journey is tedious and we feel overwhelmed by our weaknesses and failures and by the many things we need to do. In the midst of all of this, God invites us to draw aside. God asks us to acknowledge our sins and to lay down our burdens. The Great Lover reaches out to embrace us and to pour healing into our wounds. God also welcomes our complaints and struggles. The closer we are to God, the more easily we can come with all of our concerns. The more intimate the relationship, the more readily we can open our hearts.

REFLECTION: *If we haven't learned to unload our cares and concerns at the right address, we will carry unnecessary burdens or expect help from the wrong quarter.*

Victorious faith

'The church is a community that cares for the weak,
but is built on a victorious faith.'

Vishal Mangalwadi

The community of faith is to walk in the footsteps of the Master. This involves proclaiming the good news of the kingdom, healing the sick and caring for the poor. This focus on the needy is not a sign of the weakness of the church, but demonstrates its true power When the church identifies with the poor, this means that it has overcome its own self-preoccupation. When the church serves the poor, it is building a new world amidst futility and despair. And in building the church of the poor, it gives the poor dignity and the power of self-determination. For the church to serve in this way means that it must be empowered with faith, perseverance and the Spirit.

THOUGHT: *To care for the weak is not a sign of weakness, but a demonstration of love. To empower the poor is not a sign of futility, but a sign of the kingdom.*

Contemplatives

'[We are] contemplatives in the heart of the world,
twenty-four hours a day.'

Mother Teresa

There ought to be a link between spirituality and
action. Action is sustained through spirituality;
and spirituality is authentic when it is expressed
in costly discipleship. Whether we belong to a
religious order or are laypersons, we are called to
carry the Christ whom we meet in the place of
prayer, into the busy streets. And whether we are
targeting a particular needy group or are serving
in ordinary occupations, we are called to bring
the love and light of Christ. The key impulse to
all of our service is prayer. But we don't only
pray first and then work. We also pray while we
work, for in our service we seek not only to help
and empower, but we also seek to bring the
presence of Christ.

PRAYER: *Lord, may all my serving be motivated by
your love, not simply by duty or compulsion.* Amen.

Institutional renewal

'Even those structures which are most effective and reasonable to begin with always become intolerable after a while.'

Dom Helder Camara

We are social beings who create institutions: political, economic, medical and recreational. The list is endless. Most institutions have a service role in society. The church and the organisations which it spawns are also service institutions. Sadly, not all services provided by the state or the church are available to all. Some services are elitist. Sometimes institutions lose their way. They no longer effectively serve the people for whom they were created in the first place. Institutional renewal is, therefore, a necessary part of life. This work of renewal should always be our first option, rather than immediately creating new structures.

REFLECTION: *Over time, the structures that we create can become oppressive. We are, therefore, called to be change agents within our institutions.*

Wealth creation

'Wealth creation must be conceived as the God-or-dained means by which everyone's basic needs for a dignified life may be met.'

David Lim

We are called to work. Part of our responsibility in daily labour is to shape God's world. Another important feature is to express who we are and to develop our gifts and abilities. But work has everything to do with providing the necessary resources for living. Through work, we gain the means by which to provide for those in our circle of responsibility. While this circle includes our own family, it also involves others who are in need. Therefore, work should provide more than mere subsistence. It should provide a quality of life that also allows us to serve and empower our neighbour.

THOUGHT: *While in the First World there are safety nets for those out of work, in the Third World, for many it is work or starve. Yet, frequently work is not adequately compensated. This raises the issue of just wages.*

Endurance

'He [Jesus] says that he's patient and humble of heart, not because he was submissive to oppression, but because he was able to endure in that struggle.'

A teacher in the village of Papaturro

There is nothing passive about Jesus. He certainly did not take a fatalistic approach to life. Instead, he acted into life with a purpose that was empowered by his vision of the kingdom. Jesus proclaimed a new way of life and confronted the powers of darkness. These powers not only manifested themselves in sinful and broken lives, but also in the oppressive religious system of the day. In healing people and opposing the *status quo* he won friends and gained enemies. But he persisted in his work, even to the end. The faithful Son of the Father gave his life and made a way for us also to work for reconciliation and to overcome oppression.

PRAYER: *Lord, help me not to cave in to the forces of evil in our world. Help me to be faithful to you and to overcome evil with good.* Amen.

A passion for justice

'I passionately believed in the gospel of God's redeeming grace, but I was not prepared to accept an other-worldly spirituality that ignored social inequalities and allowed rampant racism.'

Caesar Molebatsi

Some Christians emphasise proclamation. Others major on social justice. We are called to do both, for we follow in the footsteps of the Man from Galilee. Jesus had a passion to see men and women liberated from their shame and guilt. But he also cared for the poor and resisted the oppressive powers of his day. He empowered the poor, but also cleansed the temple. He built a new community of faith which welcomed the marginalised. But he also confronted the religious leaders of his day. To follow Jesus is to continue his mission. To love Jesus involves obeying him. To call him Lord includes serving him by empowering the poor.

MEDITATION: *Mercy heals. Justice confronts. But justice also heals when structures that reflect God's good begin to operate within society.*

The problem of prayer

'One of the first temptations is to abandon our personal prayer.'

Segundo Galilea

Prayer is the lifeline of the Christian because it expresses one's relationship with the God of mercy and grace. As such, prayer is the joy of the Christian life. But prayer is also problematical. This occurs when our dreams remain unfulfilled, our plans are unachievable and difficulties seem to win the day. And we begin to wonder whether God has turned a deaf ear to our cry. At such times, it is easy to abandon prayer; to become angry; to be full of self pity; to complain. Sadly, this response only shows how fragile our relationship with God is and how much our happiness with God is based on blessings. Clearly, our relationship with God needs to develop a more solid footing.

THOUGHT: *The continuity of prayer, even during the dark night of the soul, is prayer that loves God no matter what is happening to us.*

A second conversion

'The slum experience had shaped their spirituality, altering values, attitudes, relationships with the institutional church. . . work, recreation. . . prayer. . . and their doctrinal stance.'

Katherine Gilfeather

Embracing the grace of Christ is a life-changing experience. Leaving one's middle-class lifestyle to work with the poor is a further life-altering experience. In fact, for some it is like a second conversion; for life with the poor calls everything into question. Not only our values, but also our theology and spirituality need to undergo significant changes, for work with the poor is much more the journey of pain and struggle than one of victory. If things don't change, then one cannot last in this kind of work. Since one needs to be sustained and nurtured in a totally new situation, an appropriate spirituality will need to provide the fuel for the journey.

MEDITATION: *In the midst of oppression and injustice, the God of hope and the God of suffering will need to be our friend. And in solidarity with the poor, we work together seeking that God will lead us forward.*

Dreams

'Those who do not have dreams and visions drown in a settled world.'

Rubem Alves

We are embedded in the world. We are sustained by it and socialised into a particular culture with its distinctive values. We experience both the beauty of our world and its pain and oppression. Yet, we also dream about new possibilities. While the present is important and needs to be celebrated, it must not have the final word. And even though we cannot always clearly see the contours of the new, we need to commit ourselves to the journey of faith; the uncertainty of risk; the commitment to act; the vulnerability of hope; the challenge to try; the work of cooperation; the need to pray. True freedom moves us to grasp the future — and the impulse of the heart is to soar beyond the present.

REFLECTION: *The dreamers of the world may be escapists. They may also be the seers of a new tomorrow.*

Union with God

'The search for union with the Lord governs the entire process of liberation and constitutes the very heart of this spiritual experience.'

Gustavo Gutiérrez

To be one with God is the quest of all Christian mystics. It also should be the quest of every Christian. To be one with God is not some merger where the one dissolves into the other. We will always be creatures. God will always be the Wholly Other. Yet, in Christ we are brought close to the Father's heart. God's Spirit indwells us and, as we pattern our life on Jesus and follow his instructions, our life will be shaped more and more like his. Union with the Lord arises out of faith, is empowered through Christ and is made experiential by the Holy Spirit. But finally, it has everything to do with the walk of obedience, where we gladly do whatever God asks of us.

PRAYER: *Lord, you are my dwelling place; the central impulse of my life; the One by whom, through whom and for whom I want to live.* Amen.

The suffering God

'God in pain is the God who resolves our human pain by his own.'

Kazoh Kitamori

While God does not prevent every pain, he is not immune to our pain, not the unmoved one. God is not unconcerned about our needs and struggles. Instead, he hears our cry and enters our pain. God has heard our cry so clearly that he has taken our sins and our burdens upon himself. In Jesus Christ, God became the one who suffers. In suffering on our behalf, he has made possible the way of freedom and deliverance. The suffering God does not only provide understanding and sympathy; he also provides liberation, for he has carried our shame, sicknesses and sorrows and offers us the gift of life.

MEDITATION: *In the God who is bowed down with my guilt and shame, I see the God of love who carries me over the abyss into eternal life.*

Cry freedom

'When the church hears the cry of the oppressed, it
cannot but denounce the social structures that give
rise to and perpetuate the misery from which the
cry arises.'

Oscar Romero

No matter how weak or how strong the voice of the
church may be, the community of believers must join
with the oppressed to cry, freedom. The church cannot stand idly by. It is not neutral. It is not a spectator.
The church is the seed of faith scattered into the world.
The church is the servant of the Creator God who has
given dignity to all men, women and children. The
church is the instrument of God the Redeemer who
calls all to reconciliation and peace. The church is a
signpost of the kingdom of God which anticipates a
new social reality where all are free and all are
blessed. The church cannot tolerate the degradation
of the image of God in human beings. It must raise
its voice and work for a better world.

THOUGHT: *The church must side with the oppressed
and, in so doing, it enters into the suffering of the suffering God.*

Unity

'Unity that is dictated by the powerful is not unity.
Unity at the cost of the poor and the oppressed, at
the cost of the integrity of the gospel, is not unity.'

Allan Boesak

Unity is not uniformity. And unity has nothing
to do with an ingroup mentality that excludes
the issues of the wider world by concentrating on
its own narrow perspectives. Unity insists on
seeing the bigger picture and includes those who
are normally excluded because they are marginalised or deemed to be unimportant. The
unity of which the gospel speaks is one which
brings diverse people together in the community
of believers. Around the common table of the
eucharist, rich and poor, men and women and
the ethnically diverse find the common hope of
new life in Christ. Where society divides, the
gospel brings people together.

THOUGHT: *Unity cannot be imposed. It can only
flourish in the seedbed of freedom and compassion.*

Crisis

'A crisis is a judgment that brings out the best in some people and the worst in others.'
The Kairos Document: South Africa

Some regard a crisis with great despair. They see it only as a problem. The situation is out of control. Crisis is virtually synonymous with utter defeat. But a crisis is much more the time of opportunity. It is the evidence that the old ways of doing things no longer work and are no longer acceptable. Moreover, it accents that to enforce acquiescence to the present system is no longer workable. Therefore, new ways need to be found and new solutions need to be devised. This requires that we be more than reactionary. We need to be creative and courageous. We need to acknowledge our part in the failings of the old and seek God's wisdom in the creation of the new. A crisis is, therefore, the opportunity to build a better world.

THOUGHT: *The failure of the old need never be the end. It can be the start for the emergence of the new.*

Prophetic action

'It is having the courage to think and say something new and to take hitherto untrod paths.'

Leonardo Boff

Every society needs its men and women who faithfully maintain its infrastructures and its services. But a society also needs change agents, for a society needs to respond to global realities and needs to renew its own life. What is true of a society is equally true of its institutions. And the church also needs to be maintained and changed. Sadly, many of us are resistant to change and we don't welcome those in our midst who have a vision for the new. Prophets, therefore, need to be doubly courageous. They need to have the courage of their convictions and they need to overcome the negative reactions of their peers. But even more is required. Prophets and visionaries cannot only point to the new; they need to bring the new into being.

MEDITATION: *To be a change agent I need to see the problems of the present; I need God's vision for the new; and I need the courage to overcome my fears, possible rejection by others and to walk my talk.*

Communion

'The human being is someone in quest of communion, someone in the process of the creation of communion.'

Arturo Paoli

We have been created for community, for fellowship with God and for brotherhood and sisterhood. Life becomes meaningful in solidarity with others. Life becomes dysfunctional when we simply live for ourselves. Christ brought a new community into being that affirmed women, welcomed outsiders and embraced the poor. His community celebrated reconciliation, dreamed of the kingdom of God, shared resources, healed the sick and brought hope to the marginalised. We are called to carry on this vision. More than building religious systems and institutions, we are called to build community where we are embraced, affirmed, cared for and empowered to change the world.

PRAYER: *Lord, thankyou for your welcome and embrace and for the gift of the community of faith. Help me to build community in my family, neighbourhood and place of work.* Amen.

The elusive Jesus

'Just when we think that we know him [Jesus], he
appears in another way.'

Segundo Galilea

Every age has attempted a stylised image of
Jesus. In one era, he was the glorious king. In
another, the man of beard and sandal. Some see
him as the idealist who dreamed about the lilies
of the field. Others see him as the passionate advocate of justice when he drove the money
changers out of the temple. But, however we see
Jesus as Son of God and Son of Man, he is bigger
than our ideas. He is both strong and gentle. He
comforts and corrects. He empowers and humbles
us. He accepts and transforms us. He forgives
and calls us to a life of obedience. There is nothing predictable about Jesus. But that he gave his
life for us is beyond question and that he came to
save the world is a truth that needs to be
embraced.

THOUGHT: *Jesus comes to us in his otherness and
makes us into the people we were destined to be.*

Energy

'There are individuals who even at low tide work the miracle of seeming always to be at high tide.'

Dom Helder Camara

There are people who have the ability to keep going even when everything seems to be against them. There are those who display courage while others are fearful. And there are those who quietly persevere while others have lost hope and interest. Such people inspire us. They can move us to try again or to 'hang in' in difficult circumstances. They can bring out the best in us. But they can also drive us to guilt and frustration. We can incriminate ourselves with, 'Why are we not like them?' Rather than the unproductive way of recrimination, we need to learn the gentle art of appreciation. God gives people in the journey of life to bring out the best in us. Instead of being jealous of them, we need to accept them as God's gracious and challenging gift.

THOUGHT: *Those who are wiser, stronger, more energetic can inspire us to do better.*

Progress

'The measure of a society's progress is not whether it can give more to those who have more, but whether it can provide enough to those who have less.'

David Lim

We live in an unjust world. Those who have much usually continue to prosper. Those who have little seldom make significant progress despite much of the work of community development. If changes are happening at the grassroots, they also need to be supported by changes at the top. That is why the whole church needs to be mobilised for the work of social transformation and nation-building. We need Christians at the macro-level as much those working at the micro-level. Christian legislators, economists and urban planners are as much needed as community workers among the urban poor. But these two groups can only be effective if they work in partnership.

REFLECTION: *The church is one significant institution that can bring the rich and poor together as the family of faith so that both can work together to build a better world. If the rich have never heard the cry of the poor, the former are diminished as human beings and if the poor have no relationship with those who can advocate on their behalf, they, too, are diminished.*

2 Corinthians 8: 9 **March 30**

Jesus

'Jesus' presence among the poor. . . was the presence of a poor man among the poor.'

Samuel Escobar

The Jesus we acknowledge as saviour and lord of our lives was neither a traditional holy man nor a religious. Nor was he a priest or a cleric. He certainly wasn't a theologian, a writer, or a person with social standing. He was a working-class man from an obscure town who never made it to the halls of power, except to be condemned there as a troublemaker. Jesus was a man at the margins of society who befriended the poor and needy. He was intimate with the Creator of the universe and passionate to see God's kingdom come. He loved people and

healed them and preached the good news of
reconciliation. He came in weakness in order to
empower us and give us new life.

PRAYER: *Lord Jesus, through your forgiveness I am
renewed; in your embrace I am secure; by your love I
am affirmed; through your touch I am healed; and by
your call I am sent into the world.* Amen.

2 Corinthians 4: 7–11   **March 31**

Impotence

'Inevitably, we must resolve the problem of loneli-
ness and impotence in a hostile world.'

Rubem Alves

Some Christians are glibly triumphalistic.
Others are trapped in cynicism and despair. The
brokenness of our world and our own failure
and weakness suggest that we can afford neither
options. If we mouth easy solutions, we live in
unreality. If we have lost our way, we fail to be
the light and salt in our world that God calls us
to be. Instead, we are called to humility, prayer

and active engagement. We acknowledge our vulnerability, but we don't embrace passivity. We embark on a life of prayer, but this does not lead to social inactivism. Rather, in acknowledging our weakness in the face of the powers of this age, we seek the power of God and work with creativity and perseverance, even when we know that we won't achieve all that we had hoped for.

REFLECTION: *Only those who face the world with humility and courage will persevere in the work of social transformation.*

April

. . .there are things that are contrary to the good news in Christ. At this point, church and world are in radical opposition.

Church and world

'The church has only two alternatives in its confrontation with the world: either it adapts itself to the world and betrays the gospel, or it responds to the gospel and enters into conflict with the world.'

C. René Padilla

Clearly, all those who belong to the community of faith are also shaped by their culture. Not everything in a particular culture is opposed to the gospel. But there are things that are contrary to the good news in Christ. At this point, church and world are in radical opposition. And this opposition should result not in a senseless harping on how bad the world is, but in an attempt to redeem and transform the flawed values of our society. This calls the church to faithful witness, for it must demonstrate the better way in its own corporate life before it calls the world to change.

PRAYER: *Lord, help me to affirm all that is good in the world and to resist all that is displeasing to you. And help me to work for change to make the world a better place.* Amen.

The eyes of prayer

'Prayer. . . brings our way of seeing the world, human beings and history more in line with the gospel.'

J.B. Libanio

In prayer, we turn away from the busyness, fragility and problems of our world. We do so not to escape, but to be refreshed and renewed. But in turning to God for comfort, strength and a renewed vision, we embrace the God whose face is towards the world. In prayer, we draw close to the God who has already drawn close to us in Jesus Christ. We raise our cry to the God who bore our pain. We turn our eyes to the one who embraced an awful death on Golgotha's hill. As a result, prayer always brings us back to the world, for the God to whom we pray is the one who both created and redeemed our world.

MEDITATION: *As I bring my world to God, the God who loves this world empowers me to work for change.*

Of gods and spirits

'So long as we remain within the boundaries of our biographies, we simply shuffle and reshuffle our gods and our evil spirits between us.'

Rubem Alves

No matter how enlightened that we think we are, we are biased by our history and influenced by the powers of this age. Moreover, within us lurk compulsions and perversions. It is imperative, therefore, that we be delivered by the God who unmasks us and lovingly transforms us. If God does not break the circle, we are bound to an existence that recycles the old pains and the tired solutions. We repeat our sins while we advocate noble changes. Thus, the God who is outside of us becomes the God who is alongside of us and the One who dwells within as the great transforming agent.

THOUGHT: *The God who is Wholly Other draws close to speak about the things that wholly concern us. And in the disclosure, we will never be the same.*

One in Christ

'In the early Christian communities, the character of the Jesus movement found expression in the abolition of social distinctions of class, religion, race and gender.'

Mary John Mananzan

We are, of course, most comfortable with those whom we know and who belong to our own social group. As a result, many of our churches have a membership belonging to a particular social class. We have churches for the rich and churches for the poor. The power of early Christianity, however, was such that it transcended racial and social categories. Faith in Christ drew together people whose lives normally would never touch. The miracle of the early church is a challenge for us today. In a society where deep divisions are evident, can the church be a reconciled community and so demonstrate a new way of life?

MEDITATION: *How does my faith in Christ impact on the way in which I treat the least of these brothers or sisters as if I was serving Christ himself?*

The new society

'By precept and by action, he [Jesus] showed that there is a more revolutionary way than violence to establish the society of love and sharing of the goods of the earth where each would give according to one's ability and receive according to one's need.'

Paul Caspersz

Ours is a fractured world. We are internally divided and socially in conflict. Within us hums the battle between selfishness and generosity and this is everywhere writ large in our social relationships. The division between the haves and the have nots is merely one of many painful social distinctions. Can these divisions be transcended? Yes, but not easily. To bring into being a community of equality requires both spiritual transformation and the hard work of building solidarity. This is a possibility, but it flies in the face of the current pressure to be independent and to look after oneself first.

REFLECTION: *Only those radically changed by Christ's power are capable of great sacrifices.*

The sustaining power of prayer

'I understood that in view of my decision to give myself unreservedly to God and my neighbour, it would be absolutely necessary for me to devote space and time to prayer.'

Dom Helder Camara

There are those who pray and do nothing. There are those who work hard and never pray. There are those who pray, but never see and hear the pain of the world. There are those who work for social justice, yet never seek the face of God. Why should we overcome these dichotomies? And how can prayer assist the work of social concern? The answers are simple. In prayer, we detach ourselves in order to be renewed and empowered. And in prayer, we seek a wisdom greater than our own. If we fail to pray, we may well exhaust ourselves and begin to believe in the virtue of our own achievements.

REFLECTION: *In prayer, we find both a humility regarding our work and fuel for the journey. Not to pray cuts us off from the very source of life.*

Brotherly love

'Brotherly love is so demanding and difficult because it consists not only in lending an outward service, but. . . [it] obligates us. . . pulls us out of ourselves to make us identify. . . with the poverty of the other.'

Segundo Galilea

The language of love is relatively easy. It is sometimes downright sentimental. The work of love is more difficult because it takes us beyond the things that we normally wish to do. The work of love challenges our selfishness. It draws us away from our preoccupations to hear the cry of the other. And it takes us on the road of costly involvement. The amazing thing on that journey is not simply that we have to give and go the second mile, but that we are also enriched. Thus, the work of love is never only for the other. It is also for ourselves, for it makes us into the persons that we most desire to be.

PRAYER: *Lord, enlarge the narrow and constricted areas of my life with your love so that I in turn can love others.* Amen.

Those who give all

'The ones to trust are the ones who give not just their money, but their person, those who give their lives for their neighbour.'

Arturo Paoli

The call to serve our neighbour is basically not a call to heroic individualism. Rather, it is the call to build communities of care. Why this should be the priority is fairly obvious. Helping our neighbour must not create dependency. And one-way giving will eventually cause the burnout of the giver. Communities of care provide a whole different way of serving. Such communities practice a common journey, a commitment to each other and the sharing of resources. In the practice of solidarity, one serves and is sustained, one gives and receives, one is supported and empowers others. In a community of care, one can truly give oneself.

REFLECTION: *It is easy to give things and to do so for wrong reasons. The giving of oneself requires relationships of care and trust.*

Confrontation

'To be truly biblical, our church leaders must adopt a theology. . . of direct confrontation with the forces of evil rather than a theology of reconciliation with sin and the devil.'

The Kairos Document: South Africa

The church is a multipurpose institution. It is primarily people centred in Christ who gather for word, worship, sacrament, fellowship and service. The church also creates secondary institutions and ministries: schools, colleges, hospitals and welfare services. The church is both a maintenance structure in society as well as a catalyst for change. The church, then, balances the work of care and that of justice. It cannot only do the former, for one cannot truly care if one is not willing to advocate on behalf of the needy. The church cannot care for the victims of oppression and exploitation, if it is not willing to challenge and change the structures of evil.

THOUGHT: *While the church is a generalist institution, it cannot be neutral. It can't be everything to everyone. The church has to take a stand and it needs to be on the side of the oppressed.*

Good sense

'Good sense is related to concrete knowledge of life;
it is knowing how to distinguish the essential from
the secondary, the capacity to see things in perspective and place them in their proper place.'

Leonardo Boff

While the Christian has an other-worldly final
destination, he or she has to make sense of this
life and to live here with purpose and fulfilment.
In order to do this, one needs the wisdom of God
and the guidance of the Holy Spirit. But one also
needs to use one's good sense. Being a Christian
has nothing to do with throwing away one's
mind. In fact, the opposite should occur. The
mind should be renewed and sharpened by faith
in God. The Christian can be realistic, critical and
discerning. But this must always be balanced by
being prayerful and full of hope.

MEDITATION: *In order to be purposeful, one needs a
sense of calling and direction. In order to be effective,
one must be determined and focussed. In order to be
fruitful, one must be prayerful.*

The work of faith

'Christian unity comes not only from a verbal confession of the same faith, but also from putting that
faith into practice.'

Oscar Romero

There are many things that can bring people
together. The reality of family. The experience of
neighbourliness. The joy of friendship. The power
of faith. The intimacy of prayer. But sharing the
common task can also build bridges of solidarity.
If our praying together never results in our
working together, then the former will eventually be weakened. For prayer leads to work and
common work leads to further prayer. Unity,
therefore, must be built at every level. We share
Christ together. We share our lives. We share
together in the community of faith. We share our
bread. We share our common joys and sorrows
and struggles. And we share in a common toil.

THOUGHT: *The sweat of our brow is minimised in
our common toil.*

The hungry Christ

'Every time you sacrifice something at great cost —
every time you renounce something that appeals to
you for the sake of the poor — you are feeding a
hungry Christ.'

Mother Teresa

In Christian thinking, there is the idea that what we
do to others we are also doing to Christ himself.
When Saul, later the apostle Paul, persecuted the
Christians, he was confronted by a vision of Christ
and the question 'Saul, Saul, why do you persecute
me?' Saul could easily have parried the question
with the retort, 'But Lord, it is not you that I am
after, but your followers.' This would have been a
very lame answer, for Saul was persecuting Christ
by persecuting his followers. The opposite is also
true — when we bless and serve the community of
faith, we are honouring Christ. And to extend that
concept one step further, when we serve the needy
who bear the image of God, we are, in fact, glorify-
ing his or her maker.

REFLECTION: *We serve God also by serving those
whom he has created.*

Discipleship

'Discipleship is rooted in the experience of an encounter with Jesus Christ'

Gustavo Gutiérrez

Being a committed follower of Jesus and being loyal to your church is not one and the same thing. This is so, because loyalty to Jesus should take priority over loyalty to the community of believers. However, when the church of which I am a member seeks to be obedient to Christ, then the two become more or less synonymous. The reason for talking about Christ and the church is to overcome the frequent emphasis on discipleship as a purely individual matter. While the genesis of discipleship is a personal encounter with Jesus, the journey of discipleship occurs in the community of believers. And even this formulation does not do sufficient justice to the fact that in coming to faith, Jesus is often mediated by the church.

THOUGHT: *The following of Jesus in a life of discipleship cannot preclude our involvement with the community of believers.*

Community of the king

'The church as the community of the king must be a demonstration of the values of the kingdom. We must flesh out what it means to love one another, to do justice, to serve others.'

Isabelo Magalit

People have many expectations of the church — and these expectations will vary from person to person. Some expect the church to provide care and comfort. Others look for intellectual stimulation. Still others primarily expect spiritual upliftment. And some people see the church as the base from which one moves to make an impact on the world. Sunday church can never meet these and many other expectations. Therefore, the church needs to be structured in small groups as well. Here people can have their more personal needs catered to. None of this means, however, that the church exists only to bless its members. The church is an instrument of the kingdom of God to change the world. But if people are not empowered, they hardly can change society.

THOUGHT: *The challenge is to build the community of believers in order to affect the general community.*

Idols of our time

'In the Bible, we discover the prophets and Jesus struggling against the same idols that dominate many of our churches.'

Jorge Pixley

The church is the redeemed community. The church is also a human institution. The church consists of people transformed by the love and power of Christ. It is also the place where the weak and broken are welcomed. The church is a counter-community where people live according to a different set of values than those in mainstream society. Yet so often the church conforms to worldly values. It has its idols in the sanctuary. These are readily identifiable: misuse of power, conformity and compromise and an inappropriate regard for Mammon. The church, therefore, must face the constant challenge to clean up its own backyard. It is called to repentance and to ongoing reformation. It is the church which walks the road of servanthood with Jesus that can call the world to forsake its idols.

MEDITATION: *The power of Mammon is broken when we become generous. The misuse of power is dealt with by a servant leadership.*

A broken world

'Given the human propensity for selfishness and personal gain, although also for justice and community, theological reflection reminds us that we cannot hope to live in a world without exploitation.'

Charles Villa-Vicencio

All men and women of goodwill long for a better world where people can live with dignity and in peace. In such a world, relationships are restored and resources are shared. Here God is worshipped and human beings care for one another. Sometimes, the hope that such a world is possible burns brightly. At other times, it is all but an extinguished, flickering flame. And so we vacilate between hope and despair. The former empowers us to work hard and try again, while despair leads us to passivity and inactivity. What should continue to fuel our hope is not the idea that we will be wholly successful, for that is an utopian dream, but that our action with God's blessing will make a difference.

PRAYER: *Lord, in the midst of our broken world you are at work bringing hope and reconciliation. May we always work with you in the task of restoration.* Amen.

Truth

'Not to look on anybody as master or slave: that seems to me the truth. The truth makes us brothers and sisters and therefore it frees us.'

Felipe, a campesino

Truth is never simply about knowing. It is also about doing. Truth, therefore, involves head, heart and hands. Truth is also not the sole province of intellectuals, for the formally uneducated may have abilities to see aspects of life far more clearly than the scholars of our time. But at the heart of things, truth has to do with transformation. Truth beckons us to practice its precepts. It calls us to abandon our previous perceptions and ideas. It welcomes us to a new way of being and acting. It calls us to leave the old and embrace the new. To embrace the truth means that we are moulding a new self. This may well lead to new relationships and new ways of acting and thus become the promise for new families, neighbourhoods and communities.

THOUGHT: *To embrace the truth particularly about ourselves and our inadequate ways of being and acting in our world means a little dying that brings with it new life.*

Sexuality and sin

'We have the tendency. . . to identify "sin" all but exclusively with a particular sort of sexual behaviour.'

Ana Maria Bidegain

Sin takes many forms. There are sins that dethrone God and practice idolatry. There are sins of deviousness and deception as well as sins of flagrant and open disobedience. Most sins, however, are sins of relationship where we misuse or abuse other people either in subtle or overt ways. Sexuality is one area of life where sin can readily make its home. Love can easily become lust and passion can become perversion. This does not mean, however, that sex and sin are synonymous. Sexuality is God's good gift which is given for our enjoyment. We should not make so much of sexual sin that it is the only focus in our pastoral concern. Sins of pride and of injustice can be equally destructive. The challenge for each one of us is to celebrate the good and to avoid every form of evil.

REFLECTION: *The grace of God leads not only to forgiveness, but also to renewal.*

Faith, love, service

'The fruit of prayer is faith. . . the fruit of faith is love. . . the fruit of love is service.'

Mother Teresa

It is never simply a matter of doing. It is much more a matter of doing what is meaningful, purposeful and helpful. But even doing the good can be done for the wrong reasons. The good must spring from good intentions and motivations. Therefore, what we do must spring from love and not from compulsion and guilt and certainly not from self-aggrandishment. This is easier said than done. Even the good often springs from mixed motives. This is where prayer becomes so important. We need God's grace to purify our hearts as we seek to help others and to transform our beautiful yet broken world.

REFLECTION: *In prayer we seek God's empowerment. By faith we see what is possible in our world. Through service we shape the world to come.*

Empowerment of the Spirit

'Far from directing understanding inwards on themselves, the experience of the Spirit launches men and women out into the world as though imbued with superhuman energy.'

José Comblin

The work of the Spirit is inward. By the Spirit, we are drawn to reflection and prayer. The Spirit also calls us to outward activity: the proclamation of good news; the pushing back of the forces of evil; the healing of the hurts of life; the building of community; and the transformation of our world. When these tasks are undertaken without the breath of God, we soon falter and fail. When we labour without faith, hope and love, we soon tailspin into discouragement. The Spirit alone can lift us to attain the purposes of God and sustain us in the journey of their accomplishment.

PRAYER: *Holy Spirit, gently carry me to the Father's heart for succour and strength and send me forth to do his will.* Amen.

Union with God

'The Christian can realise union with God not only through interior prayer, but also in action.'

Ramon Bautista

Prayer is a way of intimacy with God. In prayer, we unburden ourselves, we voice our thanks, we make our requests and we celebrate God's grace and mercy. But prayer is not the only way to intimacy. Solitude and reflection are other ways. So is service. In the service of God, we seek to bring healing to our broken world. In this task, we join God in the task of reconciliation and restoration. Thus, there are many ways in which to deepen our relationship with the Great Lover. These encompass head, heart and hands. These involve celebration and silence, creativity and reflection, and being and doing. In fact, since God shares his life with us, we too should bring our whole selves to the quest for intimacy.

THOUGHT: *Being one with God has to do with a relationship sustained by the Spirit.*

Faith and commitment

'Faith then is taking the stance that Jesus takes.'
Vinay Samuel

For some, faith is merely making a mental assent to certain tenets of the Christian faith. For others, faith is an easy believism that God will turn a blind eye to our mistakes and somehow reverse all wrongs. But faith involves so much more. Faith embraces the grace and promises of God, but it also links us to God's concerns. Faith draws us into the ambiance of God's passion for a better world. Faith calls us to follow Jesus and to embrace his vision for a kingdom of reconciliation, friendship, economic sharing and justice. Faith, therefore, is never weak. It is not escapist. Instead, while faith relaxes in the grace of God, it also strenuously embraces the vision of God for peace and justice.

PRAYER: *Lord, often my faith is convenient and cowardly. Please make it bold and proactive.* Amen.

Building the new

'[We are] building a world in which persons are more important than things and in which all can live with dignity.'

Gustavo Gutiérrez

At the heart of Christianity is an eschatological dream. Its major contours are that one day God will usher in a new heaven and earth. Then pain will be no more and all wrongs will be righted. In the meantime, we live in a beautiful yet marred world. We enjoy life, yet we are distressed by its pain. We celebrate the good and are appalled by blatant injustice. These dichotomies call us to strenuous activity. We cannot idly stand by while evil triumphs. Instead, we dare to grasp the future and begin to build the new no matter how much we falter along the way.

MEDITATION: *The places of pain need not be the places of despair. The opposite can be the case. Pain can be a trigger for healing and part of the renewing process.*

Belief and action

'Orthodoxy has to be accompanied by orthopraxis.'
Leonardo and Clodovis Boff

What one believes inevitably expresses itself in the way one lives. If one believes that God is merciful and forgiving, then clearly one needs to be generous in extending forgiveness to others. If one believes that God is just, then it is appropriate to be passionate about justice issues. Every Christian doctrine has practical implications; even that of the Trinity signals the call to community. The challenge, therefore, is not simply to believe, but to be bold in living out one's faith. It is those who believe and act who will make an impact in our world. This calls for faith and courage, for in acting we nail our flag to the mast and confront the powers of evil with service born out of hope.

THOUGHT: *The one who acts may well set something in motion that may bring about significant change. The one who fails to act changes nothing.*

Generosity

'True generosity belongs to that level of realities
that turns outward, in the direction of the other.'

J.B. Libanio

Generosity recognises the need of the other and
responds accordingly. Being generous, however,
does not necessarily mean that we become self-
forgetful. It simply means that we recognise our
partner, neighbour or foe as someone we want to
bless. Thus, generosity has nothing to do with
paying what we owe someone. It is not making
amends or settling an old issue. Instead,
generosity is an act of extravagance. It is giving
what is undeserved. It is doing what is uncalled
for. It is the surprise. It is expressing to others
God's generosity toward us.

MEDITATION: *In reflecting on the much that I have
so undeservingly received, I dare to be generous
towards others.*

Taking a prophetic stand

'Christians find their inspiration in the ideal of the righteous ruler and the legislation relating to the sabbath year and the year of jubilee. . . along with the courageous exposure of wrongdoing in high places by the prophets.'

C. Laksman Wickremasinghe

Scripture affirms the good in our world. It also calls into question what is ugly and unjust. But the Bible also contains a vision of how wrongs should be righted. It knows the language of reconciliation and forgiveness. It also knows the theme of restitution and recompense. The prophetic call for justice is not simply about righting wrongs, but is concerned with building a new world where all can be at peace with God, in community with their neighbour and live with dignity and hope.

REFLECTION: *The prophetic word rattles the cage of our comfortability and shakes us lose from our ready acceptance of the status quo.*

Inner and outer change

'It is useless to dream of reforming the socioeconomic structure. . . as long as there is not a correspondingly deep change in our inner selves.'

Dom Helder Camara

Some dream and work for a new political order. Others preach the gospel of peace with God. Often these two visions remain separate and distinct. But they need to overlap. Personal change can lead to a new way of being family and changed individuals can lead to changed communities and neighbourhoods. The more profound the change at the personal level, the more the work of social change becomes a possibility. This is particularly so when we are changed into the likeness of Jesus Christ who lived, died and rose again in order to bring into being a whole new way of life based on reconciliation, equality and justice.

THOUGHT: *In becoming a follower of Jesus, I am out of step with the dominant values of our world and I work to see more of God's kingdom manifest in our social order.*

Levels of Commitment

'In any community or association, members participate in different degrees according to different levels of self-identification with the group's values, goals and motivations.'

Segundo Galilea

While community is based on the ideal of fraternity and equality, community should never wear the mask of uniformity, for community becomes meaningful and upbuilding when it encourages diversity. Diversity recognises differing gifts and abilities amongst its members. It also acknowledges differences in social status. And it is realistic about different levels of commitment. Hence, the strong and the resolute need to encourage the weak and wavering. Yet the latter also need to make their contribution and should not be regarded as second-rate members.

REFLECTION: *Community is always fragile. It needs to be built again and again.*

Family

'We were a close-knit family that cared deeply for one another, wanted the best for each other and desperately wanted to do better than the previous generation.'

Caesar Molebatsi

Families of poverty are often families of care where the members work to benefit each other. This willingness to pull together is not characteristic of First World families where members are more concerned with personal development. But the challenge facing all of us is to build community not only in our churches and neighbourhoods, but also in our homes. Community in all these forms holds the promise of a rhythm of life that seeks the blessing of the other without self-negation. It affirms mutual service and sharing. It celebrates the use of our respective gifts and talents as both an affirmation of the self and as the vehicle to bless the other.

REFLECTION: *If we cannot build families of love and service, we can hardly build a better world.*

Giving

'Give until it hurts, because real love hurts.'

Mother Teresa

There are people who have an inordinate need to give. They give in order to find affirmation. Such giving often leads to disappointment. While giving may well provide the giver with lots of joy, giving has the other in view rather than oneself in focus. Others may be most reluctant givers. The reasons for this may range from shyness to stinginess. These hindrances need to be overcome, for not to give is a sure way to starve one's personal growth. Giving lies at the very centre of our moral universe. God gave his Son. Jesus Christ gave his life for us to win for us redemption and freedom. In having been touched by the finger of God, we cannot but give in the way that God has so graciously given to us.

MEDITATION: *Where are my limits to generosity and how can I be freed to serve and give?*

May

...we should pray and work that our institutions
in particular and society in general will reflect values
that honour God, care for the individual, build community
and uplift the poor and needy.

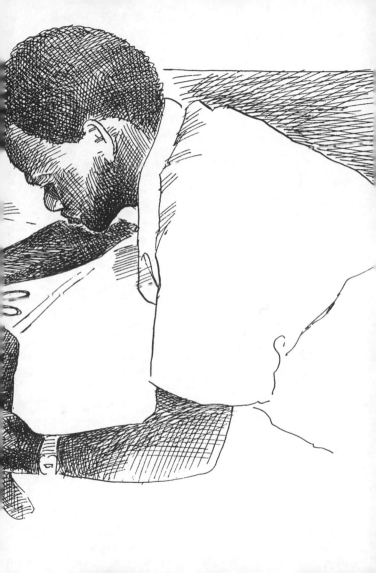

The greater good

'We are obliged to restlessly strive for a morality higher than what any particular society is able to attain at any particular time of its history.'

Charles Villa-Vicencio

It is possible for women and men to live moral and upright lives in an immoral world. There are people who are able to stand against the tide. They are able to live by the sound of a different drummer even in an organisational culture or social environment which is characterised by injustice. But our goal should not solely be to produce such heroines and heroes. Instead, we should pray and work that our institutions in particular and society in general will reflect values that honour God, care for the individual, build community and uplift the poor and needy. In seeking to fulfil the work of nation building, we must make sure that it is the kingdom of God and its righteousness that inspires all our endeavours.

PRAYER: *Lord, the good that we achieve will only be partially effective unless you make it into the greater good.* Amen.

Oppression

'Our leaders gain freedom only to turn around and oppress the people who supported them.'

Jean-Bertrand Aristide

One of the worst forms of betrayal is to be misused by those who have spiritual oversight and pastoral responsibility. The misuse of one's spiritual vocation and the perversion of spiritual power are sins against the people of God that can bring terrible confusion and hurt. Our submission to human leadership, therefore, should always be conditional. While our commitment to God should be total, human leaders should be respected because they fulfil God's ministry. When they fail to fulfil their ministry responsibilities, they themselves should receive ministry in order to be healed and restored. It is important, therefore, that our faith is not in our leaders, but in the God of grace who alone can keep them and us. Moreover, we should pray for and challenge our leaders to be open and vulnerable so that they can truly serve those under their care.

THOUGHT: *Leaders who fail to deal with their own weaknesses and pain often fail to deal carefully with the struggles of others.*

Alternatives?

'Can the present structures of our churches be redeemed from within, or must alternative parallel structures be developed?'

Vinay Samuel

The church is the people of God. Therefore, it must always be a dynamic institution. However, institutions can also fossilise. They can become unresponsive to the very people they are meant to serve. Such institutions can be renewed. A renewed faith and a renewed vision of the church's purpose in the world can trigger significant change. Such a vision can reassert that structures are never ends in themselves, but are meant to serve the mission of the church. Moreover, a church that lives beyond itself is a church that is empowered. While we may understandably become frustrated by the church's frequent lack of responsiveness, a praying and serving core group can be used by God so that the church's doors are flung open to receive both the Spirit of God and the heart cry of the world.

PRAYER: *Come, Holy Spirit, renew the creation, but particularly your people that they may live as blown along by the very breath of God.* Amen.

Galatians 6: 1–5 May 4

Challenge

'If we want to go deeper, however, desiring that as God's people we will grow together towards maturity, we must care enough to confront.'

Isabelo Magalit

Being accountable to one another is an essential element in being a Christian. This does not mean that we interfere in the petty issues of another's life. Rather, it means that we encourage each other in the walk of faith. It means that we pray for one another and support each other in the struggles of life. But it also means that we are prepared to lovingly challenge each other. True love is more than a passive acceptance. It also involves an active engagement. Love cares enough to confront. This is so important, for we all have our blind spots and our weaknesses and fears. The challenging voice of the other can turn our lives around or arrest us on pathways that we should not take.

THOUGHT: *A true friend cares enough not only to affirm, but also to challenge.*

Prophetic evangelism

'The power of prophetic evangelism is the power to bear courageous witness to the truth and accept persecution from those who are committed to suppress the truth with unrighteousness.'

Vishal Mangalwadi

Jesus was not a man for all seasons, nor did he attempt to fit in with everyone's expectations. Jesus, instead, walked the narrow road of the kingdom. He pleased his Father in heaven. He proclaimed good news. He healed the sick. He sided with the poor. And he confronted those who were the shepherds of Israel, but who failed to lighten the burden of the poor and oppressed. Jesus' followers can only walk the same road, be empowered by a similar vision and motivated by a similar passion. Sadly, we are often quite uncourageous and given to compromise. We are people-pleasers and often fail to take a stand on issues that require that we be resolute. Therefore, so much still has to happen within us so that we may reflect a much greater Christlikeness.

PRAYER: *Lord, as a follower may I walk much closer to you and be guided by the things you said and did.* Amen.

A way of life

'Conduct reflects at once a manner of thinking and a manner of acting — in short, a way of life.'

Gustavo Gutiérrez

A true spirituality involves head, heart and hands, and each of these is equally important. Our intellect needs to be converted so that we desire to think God's thoughts after him. The passionate centre of our being needs to be refocussed so that we desire to please the Great Lover who has embraced us by his grace. Our way of acting in the world needs to become radically different, since we now wish to please God, serve our neighbour and build up the community of believers. All of this suggests a radical reversal. The move from selfishness to God-centeredness and concern for others reflects a set of values out of step with the dominant ethos of our age. This way of living may seem archaic to some and downright stupid to others. But no matter how much this world may trumpet the 'virtue' of selfishness, since it is out of step with the heartbeat of God, it will only lead to futility.

MEDITATION: *I would rather follow the 'foolishness' of God than the 'wisdom' of this world.*

The bread of unity

'I think the true food he [Jesus] was bringing was
union among all people — love. He wasn't coming
just to multiply the rice and the kidney beans.'

Oscar, a campesino

Jesus preached good news. He healed the sick and
drove out evil spirits. He fed the multitudes with
bread. In all of these activities, Jesus was promoting
the kingdom of heaven. He was bringing about
peace and reconciliation and building the new community. All were welcome in this community: the
rich and poor, men and women, the socially acceptable as well as the outcasts of society. But in this
community, the terms for reconciliation were not
determined by the well-to-do. Those who were
powerful did not control this community. In fact,
they were only welcome if they embraced a servant
leadership and were prepared to serve the least of
the brothers and sisters as if they were serving Christ
himself. The church is called to be such a community
and to the extent that it isn't like that, it too is called
to repentance.

REFLECTION: *Jesus brought more than bread. He
was the bread of life and his death brings into being a
community based on servanthood and equality.*

The sin-bearer

'To understand sin is to take sin upon oneself.'
Jon Sobrino

Jesus is the great sin-bearer. He bore our sins in his own body, took our shame and guilt and brought us freedom and peace. But like Jesus, we too are sent into the world to absorb the pain and degradation of others. We do this when we pray for those who no longer desire to pray. We demonstrate this when we provide counselling, support or hospitality and friendship for those who are in personal difficulties. And we most significantly carry on this ministry when we embrace 'evangelical poverty' — that is, when we choose to live with the poor for the sake of the gospel. In sharing our common lot with the poor, we enter into their pain and poverty. In making their condition our own, we struggle with them in the hope that God will bring liberation in the midst of all our combined efforts to improve the quality of life and see justice spring forth.

REFLECTION: *Incarnation involves downward mobility and participation with those who struggle for life in the midst of death.*

Love of God and neighbour

'Only the faith that leads on to love of God and love
of others is the faith that saves.'

Leonardo and Clodovis Boff

Faith embraces and believes the words of God
and the provision of God. But faith is also an active response to God's grace and provision. Faith
doesn't only say 'thank you' for blessings
received; it also says, 'Lord, I want to please you
in everything that I do.' Faith, therefore, knows
how to joyfully receive. It also knows how to
give sacrificially. Faith looks upward to God, our
gracious beneficiary. Faith also looks sideways to
family, friends, neighbours and strangers. The
upward glance of faith seeks God's help. The
sideways glance of faith seeks to empower
others. A faith that only sees the face of God, but
is deaf to the voice of the stranger in need, is a
faith that needs to be converted, for so often God
calls us through the unfamiliar voice.

REFLECTION: *Faith, the gift of God, draws us to God
and to the needs of the world.*

Emergence of the new

'It begins with a resolution of the will, with an interior act of decision. Little by little, it becomes a part of us through the continual exercise of choices.'

J.B. Libanio

The good and worthwhile things in life do not usually fall into our hands ready made. This, of course, is not to suggest that there are not the surprises of the Spirit. There are good things that come our way which have nothing to do with our own work or striving. But in much that happens, we also play a part. We hear God's call and we respond in obedience. We make the journey where that call takes us. We meet obstacles and disappointments, yet the vision continues to burn brightly. And step by step, we not only fulfil God's purpose, but we are changed by the decisions and commitments we have made. These are then no longer motivated by the challenging voice of God, but become the very breath of our being.

REFLECTION: *When we live a certain quality of life because we want to live in no other way, then the grace of God has taken root in our lives.*

Pentecost

'Pentecost, therefore, meant power for a new lifestyle, including a new economy.'

C. René Padilla

Pentecost — the coming of the Spirit — brings
new life to individuals. Faith comes alive. Hope
is reborn. A new vision for life swims into view.
Power to serve others becomes a commonplace.
But the coming of the Spirit is not simply about
personal renewal. It also has to do with corporate
change. The work of the Spirit brings about a new
community where social and economic differences
are overcome and people live in peace and
equality. Personal and structural change must go
hand in hand. A new personal spiritual reality becomes the promise of a start to new social structures. New persons can work for better families,
renewed neighbourhoods and people-serving institutions.

PRAYER: *Lord, send your renewing Spirit upon us as individuals, but not only that; also upon our institutions.*
Amen.

Servanthood

'There is no valid leadership acknowledged in the Bible, whether it be of people or of institutions, that does not fulfil itself in servanthood.'

E.V. Mathew

Leadership is a sacred trust. Leadership is the acknowledgment by others of a person's gifts and abilities. Leadership is the opportunity to exercise those abilities with integrity on behalf of others. Leadership, therefore, provides the setting to express one's gifts in the service of others. Sadly, leadership so frequently can go wrong. Sacred trust becomes privilege and service becomes opportunism. Therefore, while leaders should pray for wisdom and ability, they should especially pray for grace. While leaders need to seek power and exercise responsibility, they especially need humility. And while leaders need to be decisive, they also need openness and flexibility. Instead of the voice of complaint, God's people need to raise the voice of prayer on behalf of their leaders.

THOUGHT: *Those who aspire to be leaders seek a noble task which frequently involves walking a lonely road and performing a balancing act between doing what is best and what people want.*

2 Timothy 1: 6–7   **May 13**

Transforming our institutions

'When you are trying to revitalise the institution itself from within. . . you will risk being misunderstood. However pure your intentions, you will look like a rebel.'

Dom Helder Camara

Institutions, like people, go through their particular life cycle. New institutions often reflect a dynamism and creativity. Older institutions can be tradition-bound and unresponsive to changing times and new circumstances. Such institutions need to be revitalised. But the work of transformation is seldom easy. People become familiar and comfortable with the way things are and resist change, seeing it as an unwelcome stranger rather than a welcome guest. Therefore, those who work for change require both courage and determination. They need to use wise strategies and be endowed with a patience that knows how to continue in the face of resistance. Those who work for change need to embrace the cause above that of their own reputation. And as such, they are a most precious gift to an institution which has become tired and moribund.

THOUGHT: *Even when change is so urgently needed, it may still be ardently resisted. Therefore, the genesis of change is the acknowledgment of its necessity.*

Psalm 78: 1–7   **May 14**

The long march

'Christian spirituality responds to the. . . longing of the human spirit. . . to march toward solidarity, justice and fraternity.'

Segundo Galilea

Deep inside of us most of us know better. We

know that the desire to live beyond ourselves and to serve others is better than to live merely for ourselves. We know that to work for peace is better than the easy road of confrontation and violence. We know that the gentle ways of God are better than our own restless striving. But so often, we crowd out the authentic voice within. We fail to still our restless senses and we do what most readily comes to mind. In fact, we frequently do what we know is not the best. This is our greatest loss. The way of reflection is too time-consuming and the way of integrity is too costly. Thus, we settle for the convenient and promote that which is least demanding and, as a result, we live with the hollow ring of our own regrets. Therefore, we need to be converted — not to embrace something new, but to do what is already deep inside of us.

MEDITATION: *The voice of the Spirit resonates with the ways of Jesus and reverberates with our having been made in the image of God.*

Holiness

'Holiness isn't a luxury reserved for only the few,
but a simple duty for all of us.'

Mother Teresa

The few cannot live vicariously on behalf of the
many, for we are *all* called to live to the glory of
God and for the well-being of others. This is not
to say that some do not lead more exemplary
lives. Some do, and we can draw encouragement
from them. But in the final analysis, we *all* have
to walk a similar road. This is not to say that we
all have the same vocation. We don't. We are
called to different spheres of human endeavour.
But in the midst of all that we do, we serve the
God who has called us and we work to build a
gentler world. In doing that, we are challenged to
serve those most vulnerable and in need. While
this may mean a spiritual vocation for some, it
means a secular vocation for many, but one that
nevertheless truly serves the other.

THOUGHT: *Holiness separates us to God in order to
serve the world.*

Affirmation

'We all blossom in the presence of one who sees the good in us and who can coax the best out of us.'

Desmond Tutu

Christians cannot afford to be naive or gullible. They are to be realistic, but also full of hope. And it is hope that sees that which is not yet, but can be. Seeing the potential in others is the gift of discernment functioning at its productive best. Bringing that potential to fruition is the great challenge of every form of mentoring. This ability to encourage and to bring out the best in others is a powerful form of self-forgetfulness. The ability to challenge people to strive for the better is servanthood at its very best. Sadly, many people with great potential are never encouraged to reach for the sky. Consequently, they live meagre lives which lack fulfilment and purpose. The challenge is to find a mentor who can clearly see what we vaguely suspect and tend to disbelieve about ourselves in order that we may be encouraged to grow to maturity.

THOUGHT: *The person who refuses a spiritual guide may walk down many futile pathways only to become exhausted in the journey.*

Isaiah 55: 8–9   **May 17**

Looking through God's eyes

'The Bible has God's eyes.'

Carlos Mesters

There are words of forgiveness, reconciliation, peace and hope. There are images of renewal and restoration. There are scenes of embrace and healing. There are themes of liberation and reversal. There are theologies of grace and freedom. There are explanations for the brokenness of our world and the imperfections in our own lives. There is comfort for the bereaved; hope for the despondent; grace for the guilty; healing for the bruised; peace for the troubled; courage for the faint-hearted; passion for the passive. And everywhere in its sacred pages are the footprints of the God who has embraced us in Jesus Christ.

There is a vision for this world and an expectation of the world to come. Even the finality of death has been negated, for we are carried across the abyss into the fullness of life that God has prepared for those who love him.

THOUGHTS. *Having read and having been enlightened, we touch the secret of the universe by touching the heartbeat of God.*

Good news for all

'Can we announce the gospel in the same way to
the oppressor and to the oppressed, to the torturer
and the tortured?'

Mortimer Arias

There is a dangerous memory in early Christianity.
It is that good can seemingly be destroyed; that the
Righteous One was crucified; that evil can seemingly triumph. But there is an even more dangerous
memory. This is the cry, 'Father forgive them, for
they know not what they do.' Through the ages,
this cry has echoed and re-echoed. Whenever men
and women in anger and bitterness have sought to
retaliate and harm those who have sought to bring
harm, there has come the challenge to bless instead.
God's grace is never simply for victims, but also for
oppressors. Mercy is available for those who are
harmed and those who perpetrate evil. To forgive
our enemies is not a sign of weakness and self-negation. It is the affirmation of life for the victims and for
those who have brought harm.

MEDITATION: *In forgiving the other I free both that
person and myself.*

Obedience

'This is true obedience. . . to obey even when there is no certainty that God will provide an escape.'

Allan Boesak

The faithful Son of the Father was rejected and crucified. Our obedience is also no shield to divert pain, difficulty and opposition. We can never bargain with God — 'If I obey, you will need to bless me or my family in certain ways.' Obedience is not a means unto a certain end. It is an end in itself. I obey because I can do no other. God has called me to walk a certain road, to fulfil a certain task, to sustain a particular commitment. I do what is asked of me and what else befalls me is out of my hands. This is not a passive resignation to life. It is relinquishing my tendency to seek a reward for my obedience, rather than recognising that my obedience is already my great reward, for in walking that road I am graced by God's benediction.

REFLECTION: *To obey is to be sustained.*

The radical Jesus

'Jesus is a universal man and a free man. He breaks
with all religious, political and ideological systems.'

Alvaro Barreiro

Jesus was not a systems man. He was a man of
the Spirit. He was not a creator of institutions, but
lived for the kingdom. He was a people person,
yet was wholly committed to seeking and doing
the Father's will. He was a radical, but had no
political agenda. None of this is to suggest that
Jesus simply breezed through life as a mystic with
no goals. Quite the opposite is true. Jesus
preached good news, healed the sick, cast out
demons, built a following, shared community,
confronted the evil structures of his day and gave
his life as a ransom for many. He paved a new
way to God, started a movement that has lasted to
the present day and, by his Word and Spirit, continues to transform men and women today.

MEDITATION: *In Jesus of Nazareth, we see the face of
God. In his proclamation, we hear the voice of God. In
his healing ministry, we see the gentleness of God. And
in his death, we see the grace of God extended to all.*

Structural evil

'Sin and evil are concretely expressed not only in individuals, but also in structures.'

Tito Paredes

No matter how hard we may try to be good, we fail to overcome evil which emerges not only when we are weak and vulnerable, but also when we are strong. Our ability to spawn evil becomes embedded not only in other individuals, but also in the structures and ideologies that we create. And we generate social practices where justice is subverted and exploitation triumphs. As a result, we have evil persons sustained by an evil system. When we wish to change such a tragic state of affairs, it is necessary not only to change individuals, but also the system. In fact, changed individuals are best sustained by a changed set of circumstances. Therefore, we need to work for change at both the micro and the macro level.

REFLECTION: *The rallying cry, 'Change the individual and thereby change the world,' is at best naive and at worst false. Changing social practices and institutions are part of the task in bringing about effective change.*

Christ's lordship

'Because he is king over all of life, we may have confidence to make every human institution subject to his will and purposes.'

Melba Maggay

While we have conveniently divided the world into sacred and secular spheres, Christ's lordship knows no boundaries. This is not to suggest that the state should run the church or the church control the state. Instead, it means that no area of life is outside of God's concern. It means that all of life should reflect biblical values and all of life is to be lived to God's glory. This means that God has something to say not only about prayer and meditation, but also about economics and the arts. It means that God is concerned about relationships and sexuality; but also about justice and ecology. For the Christian, the church and the family as well as the courts and the prison system should be of concern. The grace of God can find expression in every aspect of our lives.

THOUGHT: *If God can manifest his purposes for humankind in the pain of a cross on an ugly hill, God can equally display his kindness through his Spirit in the corridors of power and the ghettoes of despair.*

Personal evil

'We have evil inside us, too, and if God tore it out right away he would tear us out, too.'

Olivia, a campesina

It is ever so easy to divide the world into the 'good guys' and the 'bad guys'; the oppressed and the oppressors; victims and perpetrators; the innocent and the guilty; saints and sinners. But we who think we are good have evil inside us, too. For us, it may not be the evil deed, but it has been the evil thought. It may not have been acts of oppression, but it has been the art of withholding. It may not have been the hand of violence, but it has been shameful denial. It may not have been the pride of power, but it has been a tired resignation and passivity that has embraced the dust and refuses to rise and cry, freedom. Therefore, all of us need the security of God's embrace, the washing of forgiveness, the oil of healing, the word of hope and the Spirit of empowerment.

PRAYER: *Lord, I too need your grace. Forgive me and make me whole.* Amen.

Spirituality

'By spirituality, I am referring to the set of practices and attitudes by which persons. . . and Christian communities express their experience of God.'

Segundo Galilea

Spirituality is much more all embracing than faithfully exercising prayer, worship and meditation. It has to do with a whole way of life. It has to do with developing a Christian mindset about life's complexity. It also involves developing a heart sensitivity to the nudges of the Spirit. And spirituality includes doing the works of service that bless our neighbour. The challenge for all of us is that our spirituality not be one-sided. Some so emphasise the Word that they neglect the Spirit. Some major on prayer and lack a concern for justice. Some emphasise the caring community, but fail to wash the feet of the world.

MEDITATION: *All of life to the glory of God! All of life touched by God's kingdom! All of life a matter of prayer! All of life an opportunity for service!*

Grace

'The good news is that God loves me long before I could have done anything to deserve it.'

Desmond Tutu

In the normal flow of life, we are seldom good at anticipating what may occur in order to take preventive measures. We are better at turning up after the event with our help and our advice. Thus, we are frequently wise after the event, seldom beforehand. Thankfully, this is not true of God. The Lord of the universe doesn't appear after it's all over, even though we sometimes question why God did not prevent a particular tragedy. But God is there beforehand. At the very beginning of time, God set before us the way of salvation and in Christ Jesus he provided the way to life. God does not react. He is proactive. God works his purposes in the world and knows beforehand the things we need.

REFLECTION: *The God of grace calls us to accept his provision which we need much more than we realise.*

The kingdom is at hand

'The kingdom is indeed at hand and requires only that we be converted.'

Oscar Romero

While there is a hidden presence of God, the signs of God's active presence are everywhere to be seen by the eyes of faith. Far from abandoning this world in its folly and madness, God continues to sustain, bless and transform all those who seek righteousness and justice. The kingdom is God's royal activity; we merely act as servants. The kingdom is the work of God's Spirit bringing renewal and hope; we merely drink of the Spirit and carry the water of life. But the kingdom never comes easily or naturally. It comes in travail. It comes with prayer. It comes when we abandon our own ways and embrace the mystery of God's way. But when it comes, it comes with power — gently overwhelming; comfortingly healing; blazingly enlightening; radically transforming.

PRAYER: *Lord, may your kingdom of peace transform our lives and may it touch and renew the very fabric of our society.* Amen.

Consciousness raising

'One cannot be critical of something of which one is unaware.'

J.B. Libanio

Knowledge can bring great joy. The joy of discovery and enlightenment can bring new depths to our being, thinking and acting. But knowledge also imparts a burden. Knowledge brings responsibility. The more we know, the greater the opportunity to use that knowledge for the well-being of others and the transformation of our world. For true knowledge gives us more than a mere appreciation of the good; it also gives an understanding of the nature of evil. We cannot celebrate the good if we do not know how to avoid evil. We cannot work to better our world if we have little idea of what is wrong in our social and economic systems. And we cannot serve the kingdom of God if we are naive regarding the ploys of the evil one.

MEDITATION: *To know is to know God in the book of nature and in the revelation of his Word. Such a knowledge of God leads to self knowledge. I know myself in the light of God's grace. And in that light I can discern the reality of evil.*

Charity at home

'It is always so much easier for us to be very kind to the people outside our own circle than to be full of smiles and full of love to those in our own homes.'

Mother Teresa

We live in a strangely fractured world.

We have kind words for the stranger;
smiles for the sometime guest.
But oft for our own the bitter tone,
though we love our own the best.

There are men with a great ministry who are abusive fathers. There are women with great creativity who have emotionally neglected their own children. Families, instead of being places of safety and care, have sometimes become places of dysfunctionality and despair. When will this madness stop? When will we begin to treasure our relationships and commit ourselves to love and fidelity? When will we abandon the quest for selfish self-fulfilment and embrace the journey of mutual care and concern and work for the common good? If we are not converted at home, we are not converted at all.

THOUGHT: *A home is not a place where one simply sleeps and eats. A home is an environment of mutual concern and care.*

Signs of the times

'I pray that we be given grace to read rightly the signs of the times, to keep up with events, to fall in with God's plans.'

Dom Helder Camara

Some people think that to be in step with God is to be out of step with the world. This is only partly true. While we need to resist the worldliness of the world, we need to recognise that God's concern is for the world, for its salvation and transformation. Thus, we read the newspaper in one hand and the Bible in the other. Thus, we prayerfully retreat to discover the wisdom of God and we actively engage with others in order to be God's servants in our world. To be in touch with the issues of our time doesn't mean that we are out of touch with God unless we relegate God to the sideline of our lives. But if God is central to our very being and we live in the midst of life, then our family, job, loving, creativity and service are all to be under God's leadership, blessing and grace.

REFLECTION: *We need to be relevant for the sake of the opportunities it provides for the kingdom of God.*

The healer

'Jesus knew where the wounds of his people were, and he set out to heal them.'

D.J. Elwood & P.L. Magdamo

Healing can occur at many levels. Spiritual healing takes place when our disconnectedness with God is restored and we grow in the grace and knowledge of our Lord Jesus Christ. Inner healing occurs when Christ, who is the same yesterday, today and forever, heals our emotional woundedness. Relational healing takes place when we are able to forgive others and work for reconciliation and peace. Physical healing is God's gracious touch that makes us physically whole. And social healing occurs when, through spiritual renewal and social activism, our homeland is transformed to more closely reflect the values of the kingdom of God. Sometimes, these healings come in separate blessings. Sometimes, they are inter-related. It should not come as a surprise when these different healings come together, for God desires wholeness for his people.

PRAYER: *Jesus, heal my brokenness and woundedness and heal our land. Amen.*

Confrontation

'The church is confronted by the same Word with which it intends to confront the world.'

Statement of the
Evangelical Methodist Church, Bolivia

The church is the community of believers that stands under the authority of the instructions of God. Those words are life-giving and empowering because they call us to embrace the good news in Christ and call us to abandon our own ways. Released from our own agenda, we are free to do the work of Christ in the world, empowered by the Spirit. This desire to change the world can only come out of being continually transformed ourselves into the likeness and holiness of Christ. As such, we go into the world with courage and humility; strength and gentleness; firmness and flexibility; certainty and openness. Having been blessed, we encourage. Having been given so much, we give ourselves.

THOUGHT: *The words God gives us need to renew us as much as they need to renew the world.*

June

Our neighbour is any person whom we meet on life's pathway and to whom we choose to give attention and care.

Loving our neighbour

'Unless we are able to see God in our neighbour, it
will be very hard for us to love.'

Mother Teresa

For many people living in large urban centres,
their neighbours have become largely irrelevant.
Life revolves around work, family and special interest groups and the demands of these is such that
there is little time left for anyone else. Consequently,
our neighbour has become a vague spectre on the
outer edges of our horizon. The gospel, however,
invites us to adjust our focus and bring our neighbour into view. Our neighbour is any person
whom we meet on life's pathway and to whom we
choose to give attention and care. It may well be
that the person to whom we give attention may
need something that we have to give. But often the
tables are turned the other way and we are the ones
who are enriched.

THOUGHT: *Our neighbour is the person who has
ceased to be a stranger and who may well become our
friend.*

Holistic ministry

'The Lord Jesus in his ministry did not split apart the spiritual and the material. . . . For some, he cured physical infirmity; for others, he forgave sins; and for others, he did both.'

Tito Paredes

To affirm that God cares for the whole person and for one's relationships and social settings is to make a powerful statement regarding the need for holistic ministry. For if God has these concerns, then we are to share them. This means that we are to work for what is good at both the interpersonal and structural levels. In other words, we want to see people blessed, but also work at changing our institutions in order to make them places of justice which are responsive to people's needs. Holistic ministry doesn't prioritise the personal above the social and the spiritual above the material. Instead, it affirms that all of life is sacred and is to be lived to the glory of God.

REFLECTION: *My worship, work, leisure and pleasure are all to be expressions of a life lived in the presence of God.*

Mutuality

'Mutuality is relevant only where partners recognise and respect each other.'

Dorothy Ramodibe

We do not want to see a world without competition and striving. A world based on a bland sameness eventually sinks to the lowest common denominator. But mutuality need not be the enemy of striving to bring about the better. In working together not simply the *better*, but the *best* becomes a possibility. The art of partnership involves a recognition of my own limitations. This is based on the idea that I have something to contribute, but I don't have everything. Partnership also involves the recognition of the other and the contribution that person can make. But, most importantly, partnership has to find a way by which both can make their contribution without the one dominating or the other being relegated to the sidelines.

REFLECTION: *The art of partnership is consolidated in the practice of partnership.*

Conversion

'Conversion pulls us out of our hiding places and takes us "where we would rather not go" in following Christ.'

Segundo Galilea

While pride and disobedience are our original sins, evasion and avoidance are our most practised wrong behaviours. We are good at rationalisation and even better at making excuses. And in the practise of this doubtful art, we become skilled at pinning blame on the wrong person. But God calls us out of this infantile behaviour. The grace of God calls us to accountability and openness. We are called to own our mistakes and to confess our sins, for this alone leads to true freedom. And it is this freedom that empowers us to walk the road with Christ in serving the needy and mending our broken world.

REFLECTION: *Conversion turns us around. It turns us away from our excuses. It links us with the concerns of the Suffering Servant to heal our broken land.*

Breaking the bonds

'That's what Jesus was going to do with humanity, untie it from its bonds.'

Felipe, a campesino

To claim that we are already free and need no healing is to work against ourselves. Instead, we should acknowledge our struggles and broken-ness and seek the healing Christ offers. Not only do we need to be set free from our stupidities and compulsions, but also from the twisted values that others have sought to impose on us. More particularly, we need to be liberated and healed from the sins of others against us. This may well involve healing from constant put downs and criticism, and from emotional, physical or sexual abuse. But there are other bonds that may also need to be broken. In countries subject to colonialism, the long trail of ethnic castration and cultural marginalisation has left a harvest of frac-tured identities. Here, also, political and psychological healing needs to occur in order to build a new national identity.

MEDITATION: *Set me free, Lord, from the many bonds that bind me.*

A new world waiting

'Nothing can be built on hate. And a whole new world is waiting to be built.'
Dom Helder Camara

The world is both harnessed to the old improbabilities and liberated for new possibilities. To put that differently, the world is both bound to the continuity of the old and open to the promise of the new. Thus, while no predictable laws charter its course, what happens in the world is certainly no random occurrence. The world can be changed and, as men and women join hands in solving particular problems, forces can be set in motion that bring about justice and peace. To build such a new world requires more than criticism and negative reactions. It requires a vision built on justice and a passion inspired by hope. More importantly, it requires an ability to walk the long road, for changes for the better have never come easily or cheaply.

THOUGHT: *Each new generation can appropriate what is good, reject what is evil and work for the world's improvement.*

Good works

'Good works. . . point back to the kingdom that has already come and forward to the kingdom that is yet to come.'

C. René Padilla

Through Christ, through the work of the Holy Spirit and through the formation of the early Christian communities, a force for good has been unleashed in the world. While the church has not always lived up to the example of Christ, whenever it has opened itself to the power of the Spirit it has brought hope to broken lives and change to our needy world. Contemporary communities of believers, therefore, look to the early church for example and inspiration and look forward in hope that a better world will emerge. The shaping of this new world will depend on Christians praying and working for change in their neighbourhoods and places of work. It will involve a commitment to serve and love their neighbour. And it will involve the awesome task of bringing justice into the institutional and political realities of life.

THOUGHT: *To do good is the key to building a better world.*

Social reality

'Reality is moulded by human beings and it in turn moulds them.'

J. B. Libanio

Life is not made up of simple and singular processes. Life is complex and, rather than consisting of neat and straight lines, life has a to and fro movement. Life is interactive and dialectic. We regularly experience this. We are shaped by our family, but also grow beyond it and in turn shape the very family that nurtured us. This is also true of the institutions in which we participate. They make an impact upon our lives. But in turn, we can also work for organisational change. None of this is to suggest that change is easy and that socialisation processes are not powerful. What it does mean, however, is that there can be a creative edge to our lives. There can be more to life than simply repeating the old and familiar. Life provides us with new possibilities. But these can only be forged by those who are prepared to take risks and follow the courage of their convictions.

THOUGHT: *The future is shaped not by the great, but by visionaries who dare to believe that the impossible is possible.*

Freedom and service

'The journey is a collective undertaking in which the Spirit of God is a moving force. It is an undertaking in which a people learns to live its freedom in the service of love.'

Gustavo Gutiérrez

The old monastic problem had to do with a spirituality of the elite exercised on behalf of the masses. However noble the intentions of the elite may have been, the end result failed to empower the common people. Today, the fresh winds of the breath of God call not for an elitism, but for a spirituality of the common people. This spirituality places liturgy, word, community building and strategies for social change in the hands of the common people. Thus ordinary people, including the poor, become the bearers of hope in our broken and unjust world. Here, the base ecclesial communities become a sign of a new way of being church as well as a new way of acting into our world.

THOUGHT: *Power to the people can be a way to build a new world from below.*

Opposing the prince of death

'To bear witness to the kingship of Christ is to pick
up a fight with the prince of death.'

Vishal Mangalwadi

In our world are the forces of life and death. The
one or the other can come from unexpected
quarters. Christians don't always encourage the
forces of life, particularly not when they have become formalistic or world-denying. And non-
Christians don't always promote the forces of
death. Everywhere there are men and women of
goodwill who work for a better world. The
presence of good or evil, therefore, needs to be
carefully discerned. But what is clear is that
whenever people work for righteousness and
justice, whether within the church, in social institutions or within society in general, they will
experience opposition. The forces of death not
only take on the face of outright evil, but also the
voice of reason, tradition and balance.

REFLECTION: *To discern evil in its more subtle
forms and to expose and resist such evil poses the
greatest challenge for our times.*

Resistance

'Those communities have been threatened, attacked. . .
but they are still defiant. . . trying to build a decent
poor man's house upon our great garbage heap.'

Jean-Bertrand Aristide

The poor live under handicapping conditions.
There is nothing fair about their present circumstances and often there is nothing particularly
hopeful regarding their future. Yet while there are
the communities of despair, most poor communities
demonstrate an awesome resistance to the forces of
death. Thus, they work extra hours for meagre pay
and do everything possible to provide an education
for their children. They will put energy into new
community projects and help build the church
among the poor. Family members will toil in distant lands as overseas contract workers and at the
end of the day nothing too much has changed. But
the cycle of life continues and the forces of death are
held at bay.

REFLECTION: *Life in unjust circumstances cannot
wait for justice to provide the impulse for life. Instead,
the impulse for life occurs in the midst of death.*

Justified by grace

'We are always justified and we are always sinners.
We depend not on our goodness, but on the gracious mercy of God.'

Desmond Tutu

In this life, perfection eludes the Christian, for sin is
ever lurking in the background and manages to
penetrate to the very centre of our being. This is not
to suggest that Christ is not Lord of our lives. Instead, it is a humble confession that sin has not been
banished to the periphery of our existence. It
manages to strike at the very heart of who we are,
what motivates us and how we act. To say that sin
strikes us in this way is not to say that we are always this vulnerable. But we are not as holy as we
would like to be or as strong in resisting temptation. Thus for the Christian, life continues to be a
struggle, with the final victory being secure in
Christ and the present journey being sustained by
God's grace and the blessing of the Spirit.

MEDITATION: *The experience of God's grace makes
us gentler creatures.*

Fit for human habitation

'We must do what God did: destroy the disorder
that corrupts life and prepare the world to be a fit-
ting dwelling place for human beings.'

Carlos Mesters

There is so much that needs to be done. But so
often, our resources are limited, our resolve is
weak and our skills are inadequate. Moreover,
we have so many pressing needs ourselves. Our
own lives are far from adequate and we are certainly not whole. Therefore, what sort of answers
can we possibly have for other people? That we
often feel like this is understandable. That we
should therefore do nothing is inexcusable.
Moreover, the idea that we can only be useful
when we are strong is wrong. We can work in
building a better world when we are vulnerable
and have limited resources.

REFLECTION: *Joining our little to the little the poor
may possess, joining to find answers rather than already
possessing them and joining to seek God's benediction
on all that we do is the sure way to move forward.*

True freedom

'The heart which has been made free with the freedom of Christ cannot be indifferent to the human longings for deliverance from economic, political or social oppression.'

Samuel Escobar

To be truly free is to be free for God's purposes and for others. Not to be free is to remain self-focussed and preoccupied with one's own needs and concerns. This is not to suggest that we can simply ignore our own needs. But a fulfilling life is not one that revolves simply around ourselves. It must include others and it needs to learn the gentle art of giving; and the best form of giving is not to give what we think is best, but to give what people really want and need. Hence, we need to draw close enough in order to be able to hear the aspirations and the heart cry of others.

THOUGHT: *In seeking to bless others, we don't want to meet their spiritual needs only, but also their social and economic needs.*

Reconciliation

'The gospel tells us that in Jesus Christ reconciliation between and community among people are possible, however different their backgrounds.'

Allan Boesak

We can rejoice in the great promises of God offering reconciliation, peace and fraternity. But we need to weep for ourselves. Our families are fractured, our churches lack community and our world is full of discord and injustice. When will the pain end and our troubled hearts find relief? Do we hope only in this life but receive only in the world to come? The answer to these difficult issues lies at the crossroads of our obedience. If we want much but don't pray; if we seek healing but won't extend forgiveness; if want community but refuse to share; if we want to change our world but can't work cooperatively — then we squander all that may yet happen in our lifetime.

MEDITATION: *Much is possible when God's concern and our obedience join.*

The church of the poor

'In order to preach the gospel truly and effectively
to the poor, the church must achieve solidarity with
the poor and become incarnated in their poverty.'
                                        Alvaro Barreiro

Identification is an idea that springs out of the very
heart of God. In Christ, God has drawn near to us,
and embraced our sin and sorrow. When we minister in the name of Christ, we can do no less. To the
hurting, the alienated, the oppressed and the poor
we are called to draw near, not first of all with our
answers and remedies, but with a willingness to listen and a desire to understand. It is only in being
with people in their struggles and concerns that
possible answers can emerge that bring about
liberation and hope. No true answers will come
when solutions are fashioned in the safety and
security of helpers who wish to do good, but have
not heard the cry of the poor.

PRAYER: *Lord, in my ministry to others, help me to
enter their world with a listening ear and a sym-
pathetic heart and a desire to work with them under
your grace to find answers. Amen.*

Caring community

'The lack of a caring community that incarnates the Word makes us more and more incapable of being heard.'

Melba Maggay

Many of us have been spiritually birthed by the gospel of individualism. The emphasis on a 'Jesus and me' spirituality has eroded the sense that the grace of God and the Spirit of God fashion us into community. It is the community of believers at worship and play, at prayer and in service to the world, that more fully reflects who God is. That is why the church is called the body of Christ. It is a representation, though never complete, of who Christ is. If the community of faith can live the gospel and demonstrate a different lifestyle, then its witness to the world will be all the more significant.

REFLECTION: *The church is more than the pulpit. It is more than the eucharistic celebration. It is also people living their lives in mutual care and serving the world.*

Changing this world

'Is it easier to think of the kingdom in the other world so as not to have to change this one?'

Natalia, a campesina

We should think a lot about the world to come, a world where there is no more suffering and injustice. In that world, God's final kingdom will be a reality. In the meantime, we live between the times. We long and pray for the world to come, but live in faith and hope in the midst of our present broken world. The promise of the future should not turn us away from the pain of our world. Instead, it should inspire us to work for change and transformation. Having received a foretaste of the kingdom of heaven through the new life that Jesus offers us, we long to see more of God's presence and power in our time. Therefore, we don't stand idly by waiting for heaven, but strenuously work and pray for God's will to do done on earth as it is in heaven.

PRAYER: *Lord, we would like to see so much more of your grace, love and justice at work in our world. Sometimes we see so little, because so little is true in our own lives. Have mercy on us. Transform us. And use us for your ministry in the world.* Amen.

Solidarity

'We call for unity and solidarity, for it is only by
working together toward a new community of
women and men that the world will witness the
coming of the new kingdom.'

Final Statement: Asian Church Women Speak

Unity, solidarity, fraternity: powerful words,
freighting powerful sentiments; evocative words,
carrying dangerous dreams; sobering words,
reminding us how far we have fallen from these
ideals in our broken, individualistic and competitive world; challenging words, driving us to the
cross of Christ for forgiveness and empowerment. In Christ, unity, solidarity and fraternity
become awesome possibilities. For in our Lord,
we are one family, the new humanity, the body
of Christ, the community of believers. And in
Christ, reconciliation and sharing become nor-
mative possibilities.

REFLECTION: *If our community building is based on
mere human efforts, it will disintegrate. If it is centred
on the grace of Christ, then the unachievable becomes
the possible.*

Conversion

'Conversion is to conform ourselves to the values that Christ taught, which bring us out of our egoism, injustice and pride.'

Segundo Galilea

Christian conversion is not first of all conversion to a set of ideas, particular teachings or certain dogmas. It is also not first of all joining the institutional church, although all of these things are very important. Instead, conversion is embracing a person — or, more specifically, being embraced by the person of Jesus Christ. And what this encounter means needs to be elucidated by the teaching ministry of the church. Because conversion is encounter, it always involves more than a change of mind and a change of ideas. It involves a change in everything that we are. This includes our emotions, plans and dreams as well as our lifestyle and our values.

MEDITATION: *Our initial conversion starts the journey of faith. Our ongoing conversion consolidates us in the journey.*

The power of love

'When you look at someone with eyes of love, you see a reality different from that of someone who looks at the same person without love, with hatred or even just with indifference.'

Desmond Tutu

Love can see things that negativity or indifference cannot. Does that mean that love merely idealises? The answer is: not necessarily. Love can see truly, for our gaze is blurred when we look at another with anger or disregard. And what love can see best is the worth, giftedness and potentiality of the other person. Thus, love has a way of unlocking what is hidden in the other person, for love provides a safe place — a place of acceptance, openness and care. In such a setting, old fears can be overcome, risks can be taken and growth can take place.

THOUGHT: *If love cannot unlock the other, nothing else will.*

Personal relationships

'We can move in the direction of justice, but if our personal relationships don't become more human, we haven't moved in the direction of the reign of God and, in the long run, we will discover that our point of arrival is just another form of tyranny.'

Arturo Paoli

It is so easy to trumpet a particular cause, particularly the cause of equality, justice and fraternity. It is more difficult to mobilise people to a cause. And it is most difficult to implement the cause in ways that truly achieve the stated and desired outcomes. But a cause can simply become another project, another job to be done. And the implementors can become so task orientated that they neglect to practise the very things they hope to achieve for others. Thus, they fail to practise community and care amongst each other while trying to impart these very blessings to others.

REFLECTION: *Build at home what you want to build in your neighbourhood.*

Community

'The beginning of a community: when the many
have the same dreams.'

Rubem Alves

The genesis of community is not found only in
organisational cleverness and the genius of community is not simply the careful application of
group skills. Community is always a gift. It occurs
where people dream the impossible dream and
believe that their vision can be realised and im-
plemented. Community emerges when people
come to a common mind and dare to begin to
walk the long journey together. As such, community is audacious. It is charismatic. It has to do
with the Spirit. When community comes about, it
is like a strong current. Its enthusiasm and energy can be boundless. But it needs to find the sustenance for its development beyond such pristine
beginnings.

REFLECTION: *Can community weather the slow but
sure forces of institutionalisation?*

The desirable

'Peace is preferable to hostility, generosity to revenge, preservation of life to its destruction, production to destruction, trust and tranquillity to threats and fear.'

José Míguez Bonino

The rather trite saying, 'Be part of the solution and not of the problem', is well meant, but fails to address the central problem. Our difficulty is that often we are both. And this is due to the fact that we are so often divided within. We want to help, but we also want the credit. We want to love, but sometimes lust. We want to produce the good, but go about producing the good in inappropriate ways. We seek to empower others, but often lapse into various forms of control. The desirable, however, does lie readily at hand, but needs to be won. It emerges out of the struggle to be obedient to God rather than to go our own way.

PRAYER: *Lord, I confess my mixed desires and motives for so much that I do. Purify me and empower me to pursue the road of righteousness.* Amen.

Gratitude

'In gratitude we give to others. But in giving we express our gratefulness to the God who gave and keeps on giving.'

Evelyn Miranda-Feliciano

To be grateful is the dynamo of life, for gratefulness is premised on the ability to receive with joy and thankfulness. It involves the recognition that, as part of the human community, we receive so much from others. And it acknowledges that no person is an island complete unto himself or herself. But even more so, true gratitude celebrates the generosity of God who gives us life, salvation, charisms, purpose and direction. Moreover, this generous God accompanies us in our life's journey and sustains and empowers us along the way. How blessed we are! And, in celebrating this fact, we can make loving service to others to be our grateful response.

MEDITATION: *I have received so much. How do I become the good steward of so many blessings?*

Action

'You become motivated to the extent that you are acting.'

Paulo Freire

It is important to think; pray; visualise; plan. But it is equally important to act; strategise; mobilise and initiate; implement. It is, furthermore, important to reflect on one's action; evaluate; reassess; refocus. Many other key concepts could be added to these three interrelated activities. But their complimentarity is self-evident. The action phase of any program or activity can be empowering or debilitating. It all depends on the success or otherwise of the program. While success can move us forward, difficulties need not stop us. They can be a goad to new initiatives. But this will require that we be flexible, open and prayerful in finding the necessary solutions.

THOUGHT: *No significant new project will be without complications and difficulties. But these need only be temporary hindrances along the way.*

Alternatives

'The church. . . cannot be content to play the part of a
nurse looking after the casualties of the system. It must
play an active part both in challenging the present unjust structures and in pioneering alternatives.'
Donal Dorr

The church is called to be the midwife of the new
order. It's a signpost of the kingdom of God. It is that
part of humanity where Christ is honoured as Lord
and Saviour and where the words and deeds of
Jesus are being emulated. This being so, the church
does not reinforce the existing order. Instead, the
church proclaims and demonstrates radically new
possibilities. These include: the gentle art of reconciliation, the difficult task of peacemaking, the passionate pursuit of justice and the joy of sharing and
celebration. The church, therefore, does not stand on
the sidelines of life to point the corrective finger. It is
in the midst of life, calling people to a new way of
living.

PRAYER: *Lord of the church, empower all of us who
belong to you to be servants in your world, bringing
peace and hope.* Amen.

Criticism

'Respect for the people's word need not mean approval for whatever they say. Any criticism becomes constructive when based on a fundamental attitude of respect and listening.'

Clodovis Boff

Insiders are usually suspicious of outsiders. Outsiders usually generalise about insiders. Yet insiders and outsiders need each other, particularly in the difficult task of reconstruction. Over time, organisations, institutions, communities of believers and neighbourhood or rural communities can develop difficulties which are blindspots for insiders. This problem does not call for the knight in shining armour to come from the outside with all the insights and answers. Instead, it calls for the art of partnership where insiders and some outsiders join in the task of listening, identifying issues and clarifying strategies for change and transformation.

REFLECTION: *The classic structure for partnership is the I-Thou relationship, where both the insider and the outsider are treated with equal dignity and respect.*

Mission

'Some. . . will emphasise mission as total availability; others will emphasise the witness of life. But in some way or other, all of them have to achieve a synthesis between living hope and bringing this hope to the lives of others.'

Segundo Galilea

Mission is service and service lies at the very heart of the Christian life. Service can take many forms. Some prioritise prayer as a form of service, particularly intercessory prayer. Others stress the importance of evangelism. Others again emphasise the work of justice. But whatever form our service may take, its purpose is to empower others by bringing them closer to the giver of life. Discovering new life in Jesus becomes the radiating centre from which other priorities can flow, be they family enrichment, overseas mission or involvement in the marketplace. While we wish to do good to people, we want to make sure that we introduce them to a way of life where God is the focus and the priority.

THOUGHT: *There are many ways in which we can bless others, but we do want them to know the One from whom all blessings flow.*

Evangelisation

'Evangelisation is not one issue among the various issues. . . [it] is itself the central issue. When we are inquiring about what it means. . . we are inquiring about the very essence of the church.'

Juan Ramon Moreno

Evangelisation is not the sole province and concern of evangelicals. Every major Christian tradition seeks to make Christ known. In the proclamation of good news; in the building of communities of faith; in the works of ecclesiastical art and religious drama; in oratorios; in the work for justice; in developing a Christian presence in the market-place; in building Christian families; and in developing a personal spirituality with a global concern: in these and in many other ways, Christians seek to make Christ known in our beautiful yet broken world. Whatever the means for proclamation, the power behind those means can only be the grace of God which alone can remove the barriers and welcome people home.

PRAYER: *Lord, may my words and deeds reflect your truth.* Amen.

July

*. . .in the midst of life with all its challenges,
obstacles and possibilities, we seek to do
not only the achievable good, but seek the source
from where all goodness comes.'*

Heart cry

'The human cry in every age is the echo of the eternal and infinite voice that beckons the individual.'

Leonardo Boff

Unless we have given ourselves totally over to evil or have become psychotic, we long for the good both in ourselves and in our world. We pray for peace. We work for justice; seek holiness; fan the flame of hope; strive to have integrity; serve with enthusiasm. And, in the midst of life with all its challenges, obstacles and possibilities, we seek to do not only the achievable good, but seek the source from where all goodness comes. Thus, in the midst of life with all its demands, we learn the gentle art of solitude and reflection. We find ways to draw near to the God who beckons us. We learn to be still in order to hear the God who speaks. We come with our needs so that we can be forgiven, healed and empowered.

REFLECTION: *God calls us to do good. Thus God seeks to make us good. And in order to be good, we need to be transformed and sustained by his grace and love.*

The body of Christ

'We're here in this church and he doesn't care about the church, as a building. What he cares about is for all of us to love him.'

Oscar, a campesina

God is hardly opposed to structures. God affirms the family, the state and the church and instituted the role of priest, prophet, apostle, pastor and deacon. But God is hardly pleased with institutionalism, where structures and systems serve their own ends. God's passion is that his people are empowered so that they will serve one another and the world for which they have responsibility. Thus, we pray for one another. We care for those within the community of believers. We challenge each other to faithfulness and commitment. And, out of the reality of our life together, we point others to the source of life in Christ Jesus and work for peace and justice in the wider community.

THOUGHT: *If love is not present within our personal interactions and our structures, then formalism and control are likely to be the poor substitutes.*

Temptation

'Temptation is neither sin nor evil, but only its means of seduction.'

Segundo Galilea

In the journey of faith, we may move from immaturity to maturity. But we never come to a place where we are beyond temptation. What may be true, however, is that temptation is more easily recognised and resisted when we have grown in our Christian commitment. But don't be too confident! Various stages of life bring their own peculiar difficulties and seductive charms. An earlier life of decadence can leave us particularly vulnerable in certain areas of our life. And circumstances of poverty and oppression, as well as that of power, status and riches, can bring their own propensities to evil. Since temptations will surely come to those who seek to honour God, the antidote is great humility and simple transparency.

REFLECTION: *Since God never tempts us to do evil, we need to seek God's help to overcome that which will pull us away from a life of obedience.*

Renewal

'Instead of being so eager to reform others, let us first make a serious effort to bring about our own revival.'

Dom Helder Camara

It is ever so easy for us to launch out into the world with our easy answers and cheap solutions. We assume that because Christ is in our hearts we can solve the world's problems. But this is far too simplistic. In order to make an impact on others, we need to become men and women of prayer. Further, we need to draw close to those we seek to help in order to respond to their real struggles. And we need the wisdom of God in the heat of the day and in the midst of difficulty in order to find the way forward. Thus, instead of being so sure and confident, we can only proceed with humility and trust that God will lead us onward.

PRAYER: *Lord, in the midst of our helping, help us. In the task of healing, heal us. In providing answers, grant us your wisdom. And in blessing others, grant us your grace.* Amen.

Faith and service

'Faith is action in love and love in action is service.'
Mother Teresa

Service so easily is seen as a duty, but it actually is a privilege. This is so for a number of reasons. First, we have the opportunity to express our natural and special talents and, in so doing, we experience the joy of pouring ourselves out in creative endeavour in the world. Here, self-expression is the focus. Second, we have the opportunity to express something of God's character. Here, witness is the focus, for true service seeks to demonstrate to others God's concern for them. Third, it is always a privilege to be able to contribute something good to another's life, family and community. Here, transformation is the focus. In the midst of the forces of death and injustice, life can be enhanced by those who seek to build a better world.

MEDITATION: *In serving, do I diminish myself or do I enhance myself and others?*

Empowerment

'We can guide the people to growth and freedom by diminishing our intervention as they begin to sustain themselves along the way.'

Clodovis Boff

The task of parents is to nurture their children to maturity so that they can take their responsible place in the family, church and world. This involves the gentle art of guidance, affirmation and encouragement and the difficult task of letting go. This rhythm of life from one generation to the next is a simple reflection of the way God treats us. He carried Israel through the wilderness in order for it to become a nation of priests. In the church, it should be no different. We are nurtured in the community of believers as babes in Christ so that we may eventually take our place as mature women and men able to teach and serve others. In community development, the pattern is similar. What a joy it is to play a part and not to take control! What a privilege to make a contribution and to see those with whom we work make their own decisions and make their own way!

THOUGHT: *Empowering others is the greatest way in giving ourselves away.*

Martyrdom

'The present-day Latin American experience of martyrdom bids all of us to turn back to one of the major sources of all spirituality: the blood-stained experience of the early Christian community.'

Gustavo Gutiérrez

The church has a long history of martyrs. One need only think of a Polycarp, a John Hus, a Dietrich Bonhoeffer. In the last several hundred years, the church in the West has produced its missionary martyrs. But now the torch has largely been handed to the Third World. A tired and decadent West with its cheap grace Christianity presently lacks the power for great commitment and sacrifice. It is now the church of the poor in the Third World which is demonstrating the power of incarnation, joy in the midst of suffering, God's presence in the face of injustice. And it is of these communities of faith that the blood of the martyrs has once again become the seed of the church.

REFLECTION: *May the church in the Third World, nurtured at the tired breast of the Western church, revitalise that which brought it to birth!*

Luke 19: 1–9   **July 8**

Worldly holiness

'Zacchaeus. . . was called to discipleship and to holiness while remaining in the world of his ordinary life.'
Thomas H. Green

The outstanding men and women of faith are not necessarily those who serve in the formal ministries of the church. Being a Christian in the marketplace is equally challenging, if not more so. The Christian in the world of business, media, politics and academia has the opportunity not only to proclaim the good news of Jesus Christ, but also to redeem these areas of life. The institutions of our land need to be both humanised and Christianised. We need to work for the common human good as well as for the kingdom of God. Thus, Christians in the workplace need as much support and care for their role in the world as others need for their role in the church.

THOUGHT: *Those serving the church are there primarily to serve the laity so that they can play a transforming role in the world.*

The light of his love

'Jesus, he's here now in this community freeing us from all slavery. We can see him shining in the unity of the community with the light they saw in him. . . the light of love.'

Rebeca, a campesina

How is Jesus present in the community of believers? Does he inhabit our programs and structures? Is he present as the Living Word in the preached word? Is he present as spiritual sustenance in the sacraments? Does Christ exist as community in the relationships of love and care among the members of the community of believers? Clearly, Christ manifests himself in many ways. But he is present only to those who seek him in faith and humility. He is there for the broken hearted. He joins the poor in their journey of liberation. He extends mercy to those who acknowledge their folly and turn to him.

REFLECTION: *When Christ is present in the midst of the community of believers, we can only marvel at his grace.*

Responding to God

'The first three attitudes, . . of the Creator-creature
relationship. . . [are] praise, reverence, service.'
Juan Luis Segundo

Our relationship with God doesn't start with
service. It begins with embrace; acceptance; welcome; forgiveness. And even when we have
made the long journey of faith, our relationship
with God is sustained by the nurturing character
of God. his amazing acceptance and this sustaining love elicits from us praise, thankfulness and
worship — and this spills over into a life of
obedience, commitment and service. Our service
can never be sustained when motivated by the
need to prove ourselves or by the desire to pay
back. Instead, the commitment to serve springs
eternal from the grace and love God has extended to us in Christ Jesus.

MEDITATION: *If I bow the knee in gratitude, I will
also say: Lord, what do you want me to do?*

The best

'We need to be. . . advancing the possible good even
as we seek the impossible best.'

Melba Maggay

Christians need to commit themselves to do the
achievable. Little is gained by having great
pipedreams. These are usually full of hot air.
This is not to say that we shouldn't be full of
hope; that we shouldn't dream the impossible
dream; that we shouldn't strive to be more creative and holistic. What it simply means is that we
need to get on with the job and do what is practical in difficult circumstances. The ideal moment
will probably never come. The perfect response
will ultimately evade us. The best plans will
probably fail to materialise. In spite of these
realities, we should do what we must, trusting
God to carry us forward.

REFLECTION: *We should never be satisfied with our
projects and programs, but open them to the inspiration of the Spirit.*

Spirituality

'Spirituality is purely and simply the actualisation
of the spirit of Jesus in our own times.'

Jon Sobrino

Spirituality has to do with certain disciplines.
These include prayer, reflective scripture reading,
meditation and fasting. But spirituality is so much
more. It is the whole of our life centred on Jesus
Christ. This involves our praying and our loving;
our worship and our finances; the practice of
solitude as well as our daily work; our concrete
plans as well as our euphoric dreams. Spirituality
has to do with the way in which the words and
deeds of Jesus have taken root in our lives. It has
to do with the way the whole of our lives are
orientated towards God and his purposes.
Spirituality involves the Spirit of God impregnat-
ing every aspect of our lives with values that
resonate with the way things are done in heaven.

MEDITATION: *To be in Christ is not merely belonging to him. It has to do with his active presence in our
lives. Can we identify the signs of his presence with
us?*

Holy Spirit

'The sinner is not only pardoned but. . . is given new life by the indwelling Holy Spirit.'

Isabelo Magalit

The heart of Christianity is the good news that God can mend a broken creation, liberate those who are oppressed, forgive those who are marked by guilt and shame and heal those who are wounded by the hurtful circumstances of life. The message of Christianity is not simply one of forgiveness. It is also one of restoration. Restored to God through faith in Jesus Christ, we can restored to ourselves, to others and to our world. This is possible, because God makes himself present to us by the indwelling Holy Spirit. It is the Spirit who gently works within us, enlightening, inspiring, correcting, beautifying, empowering. Giving more credence to our gentle and often unobtrusive Guest will enable us to live the Christian life much more authentically and powerfully.

PRAYER: *Lord, may your Spirit constantly envelop and empower me.* Amen.

Going back to the roots

'Christianity. . . is always in need of re-simplifying,
going back to its origins, ridding itself of the exces-
sive superstructure it has acquired through history.'
José Comblin

Christianity's long history displays the splendour
of the cathedral, the monastery, the oratorio,
religious art, creeds, theologies, canon law and
many forms of ecclesiastical infrastructure. At the
same time, Christianity knows the simplicity of the
desert fathers, pietist groups and the contemporary
house churches. The power of the church and the
simplicity of the church form contrasting themes
in the church's long history. Some argue that the
church's true power lies in it being the little flock,
hidden like leaven in the midst of an evil world.
Others claim that the church should use its ecclesiastical influence to make an impact on
society. This debate will not go away. But what is
clear is that the church will exercise true power
when its message and deeds conform to the good
news in Christ Jesus.

THOUGHT: *True power will always express itself in
servanthood.*

Freedom

'It is not only the freedom of the oppressed that is at
stake. . . but also the liberation of the oppressor.'
Allan Boesak

We have created a divided world — whites and
blacks, bosses and workers, those on the political
right and those on the left. We also know of the
bitter antagonism that can exist between the per-
petrator of a crime and the victim, the abuser and
the abused, and the oppressor and those who are
oppressed. And sadly, we know that the
downward spiral so often continues when the
abused become abusers and those who were oppressed in a brief moment of reversal emulate
those who had previously victimised them.
Where will this spiral stop? Surely, only in the
healing of both the oppressor and the oppressed.
And how might this take place? Undoubtedly,
when the oppressed extend forgiveness to those
who have hurt them, but also call them to repentance.

REFLECTION: *Who has the grace and courage for
these things? Only those who can look beyond their
own pain to a new world waiting to be born through
the power of reconciliation.*

Discernment

'It is a cardinal principle of discernment that the Lord always speaks in peace, even if he is rebuking or chastising those he loves.'

Thomas H. Green

There are times when God is silent and in the silence we need to discern the hidden voice of God. There are times when God speaks, but we are so busy talking that we drown out the wisdom of God. There are times when we are so anxious and driven that we equate God's gentle whispers with our own anxious thoughts. But whenever we are still enough to hear and we lay down our own agenda, God will speak to us with a loving and gentle clarity which will always surprise us. God restores with gentleness, rebukes us in love, guides us with clarity, imparts wisdom with simplicity and affirms us while correcting us.

THOUGHT: *Why do we spurn the voice of the One who alone can carry us across the abyss of our own folly and can bring us to the place of true wisdom?*

Selfishness

'Selfishness. . . feeds an insatiable hunger that first eats up everything belonging to others and then causes a creature to devour itself.'

Dom Helder Camara

Western individualism has yielded a harvest of selfishness. This is not to suggest that selfishness does not exist elsewhere; nor does it suggest that every feature of individualism is wrong. The challenge for Christians, however, in both West and East is to move beyond a selfish individualism and an equally selfish group-think and communitarianism. Christians are called by Christ to live beyond themselves or beyond the demands of their extended family. We are called to be hospitable and to open our lives to the needs of others. We are challenged to bless those who cannot return the favour. We are to help those who are weak and marginalised. In the pursuit of these things, we don't earn heavenly credit and we don't easily change the conditions of the poor. We are simply following in the footsteps of our Master, Jesus Christ.

THOUGHT: *Selfishness is like a cancer. It finally destroys. Service is like a seed that produces an abundant harvest.*

Psalm 133: 1–3   **July 18**

A new humanity

'It is the image of God in man that desires a world of brotherhood. . . The fallenness, frailty and sin of man, on the other hand, make him desire his own prosperity.'

Geevarghese Mar Osthathios

Can we build a better world when so much of life is fragmented and so much is scarred by sin? And what can we contribute when we are at best forgiven sinners and wounded healers? The answers to these questions are startingly simple. We can do little when we simply focus on the problems of our world and our own frailty. We can do even less when we have answers for others, but have found none for ourselves. And we have nothing to contribute when we have given way to cynicism and despair. But we *can* make a difference when we have been immersed in the forgiving grace of God, when we are discipled into an obedient following of Jesus, when we are healed of the wounds of the past and when we are empowered by the Spirit to bring good news and liberty to captives.

REFLECTION: *Transformed lives, families and communities of faith can be the salt, light and leaven that our world so desperately needs.*

Ecclesiastes 3: 9–14   **July 19**

Interrelated

'We see a movement. . . from knowledge to understanding, to freedom of commitment for greater service.'

Ramon Bautista

What is our final purpose? Is it celebration and worship or is it obedience and service? In one sense, the question matters little, for the two are inseparable. Worship is a form of service and service is the overflow of celebration. And that is precisely how life is! It is not a series of neatly packaged categories. Instead, it is a gentle rhythm where the one aspect of life impacts upon the other. And it doesn't matter where we turn, the same pattern is everywhere writ large. Body and soul are interrelated. So is faith and obedience. So is the individual and community. We cannot celebrate one aspect of life and neglect another. Prayer and politics, spirituality and sexuality, solitude and service all belong to the rhythm of life which finds its centre in Christ, our Lord.

THOUGHT: *In life there is the law of sowing and reaping. But sometimes we reap what we do not deserve.*

Incarnation

'There can be no evangelisation without incarnation.'
Alvaro Barreiro

The God who brings good news is the awesome and all-powerful One. This One is also the tender and caring Shepherd; the mighty One who draws close and enters our pain and struggle. This most admirably took place in the coming of Jesus Christ, the Word made flesh. We can hardly better this profound strategy. If we want to bring good news, we must draw close. We need to enter the community of the other and join them in their struggle for life and liberation. Preconceived ideas and answers we need to leave behind. New answers will need to be found in the midst of the struggle for life and hope. When the church sides with the poor and the marginalised, it demonstrates the power of the incarnation; for, as you have done these things to the least of these my brothers and sisters you have done them to me, says Jesus.

THOUGHT: *The church of the poor can only be built on the concept of incarnation.*

God's grace

'What a tremendous relief it should be . . . to discover that we don't need to prove ourselves to God.'

Desmond Tutu

So much teaching and preaching in the contemporary church is so moralistic that the heart of the Pauline message goes unheeded. In a nutshell, this message shouts the good news to all who, mistakenly and wearisomely, seek to make it all happen by their own good efforts: that God comes to us with his embrace; his kiss of peace; his forgiveness; his transformative grace. It reminds us that the genesis of the Christian life lies in the gift of new life in Christ Jesus. It highlights that the breath of God's Spirit is what carries us forward and not our striving and our endless self-justification. Touched by God's healing hand, we begin to live again. This new life, however, is not given to us in order that we prove ourselves; rather, deeply loved by God, we express ourselves in gratitude and faithfulness.

THOUGHT: *Those who have the humility to receive all that God has to give are the ones who can give to the world what it needs most.*

Jesus, the dreamer?

'John sang a funeral hymn, Jesus an alleluia verse. John refused to eat bread; Jesus broke his bread. John refused to drink wine; Jesus changed all the water in the kitchen into wine.'

Joseph G. Donders

From the perspective of a business person, Jesus was a dreamer. From that of the religious establishment, he wasn't orthodox enough. From that of the political radicals, he was far too conservative. But for those who came seeking help, Jesus proved to be more than sufficient for all their needs. For the sinner, there was forgiveness. For the hungry, there was fellowship and food. For those bound in chains of darkness, there was deliverance. For the outcasts, there was a welcome. And for the disenfranchised, there was participation in the kingdom of God. All of this was more than a dream. Lives were transformed and made whole!

REFLECTION: *If Jesus was a dreamer, I want to spread his dream.*

Comfort and challenge

'Jesus calls to himself those who are overburdened and offers them rest, but he does not blunt the cutting edge of his demands.'

Thaddée Matura

We are at best wounded healers. This is not to suggest that there is no help or hope for us while we are busy serving others. But we can't effectively serve others while we are full of our own pain. Our own lives need the touch of God's gentle embrace. Our inner ear needs to hear the whispers of God's hope and our troubled mind needs the caress of God's peace. Thus, we serve others having first tasted God's blessing and kindness. But God's grace is not meant to benefit us alone. There is to be a flow-on effect. Forgiven, we forgive others. Blessed, we benefit others. Embraced, we welcome others. Accepted, we serve others. Empowered, we equip others.

REFLECTION: *Come to that place of rest where your bitterness is lanced, your hurt is healed, your sin is forgiven and your burden finds relief. There you will find fuel for the journey of true servanthood.*

The great gift

'Yes, God loves them [the ragpickers of Cairo]. I am only a poor creature fashioned from the same clay as they, but in me lives the Breath of Love which makes me give my life voluntarily to change theirs.'

Emmanuelle Cinquin

The life of commitment, sacrifice and service is never only a one-way street, where we give to those who are in deep need. This approach is far too messianic. True service, while involving the desire to help, bless and empower others, also means that we are blessed and enriched in the process. In this way, we too are sustained and nurtured. If our service to others simply drains us and we are not enriched, then there may be something seriously wrong with our service. Jesus did not simply call and bless his disciples, but they became his friends and he both needed and rejoiced in that friendship. We can do no less. We, too, need to be befriended by the very people we seek to serve.

PRAYER: *Lord, thank you for all that you have imparted to me, enabling me to serve others. And thank you for everything that others give back to me.* Amen.

Participation in life

'The violation of a people's desire to share in the shaping of its own history means denying the humanness of the majority of the population, refusing them a share in the human condition.'

Juan Hernández Pico

Those with power, means, status, position and resources enjoy the benefits of society that are denied those at the bottom of the economic ladder. But the elite not only have much. They also have control and shape the dominant ideology of a society. But those who are less fortunate also have much to contribute. Not only should their voice be heard so that their needs can receive attention, but their struggle and pains have given them a wisdom that can enrich the common good. Insight and wisdom are not the sole possession of the great and powerful. The dispossessed also have their contribution to make. A society, therefore, impoverishes itself when it excludes the meaningful participation of some of its members.

THOUGHT: *While it is more commonly accepted that the weak need the strong, the reverse is also true.*

Taking the plunge

'A [person] can be forgiven for making a wrong decision. What is unforgivable is when fear stops him from making a decision.'

Cardinal Jaime Sin

No-one would want to claim that making important decisions is ever easy, although some people come at making decisions in less traumatic ways than others. The difficulty in decision-making is that finally we have to take the risk and live with the consequences of the choices we have made. This requires both faith and firmness, prayer and action, and hope and commitment. Finally, when things have been carefully thought about, submitted to God for his wisdom and discussed with trusted friends, we have to take the plunge, trusting that God will make a way for us. This requires a courage that we often don't have in reserve, but is given to us in the heat of the moment.

REFLECTION: *Remember some good decisions you have made and identify what made them such. Do the same with some bad decisions and identify what went wrong.*

Signs of our commitment

'We preach the message of our Lord. But the people want credentials. Where are our wounds; what are we suffering?'

Miguel D'Escoto

We should not feel too affronted when people cast doubts on our Christian message, our methods and our motivation. Sometimes our message is legalistic rather than liberative. Sometimes our methods are inappropriate or disempowering. And we all have to admit that so much of what we do springs from mixed motives. But the major factor that alienates us from those we are serving is that we minister out of strength and fail to be vulnerable and open to the contribution of others. We come with our answers, when we haven't heard their questions. We come with our help when we haven't heard what people need. We come with our resources, but fail to allow others to contribute. We come with healing for others, but fail to identify and be open about the woundedness of our own lives.

THOUGHT: *Out of our own woundedness life can flow.*

Signs of God's love

'Humans are both the object of God's love and the means to reveal that love. We exist both because of his love and in order to reveal to others his love.'

Ennio Mantovani

Blessed in order to bless; forgiven and able to forgive others; loved and extending oneself to others; cared for and caring; nurtured and able to mentor others: such is the magic rhythm of life. It is not having and holding; acquiring and withholding; gaining and keeping. This subverts the flow of life. It is receiving and giving; being filled in order to share; being blessed in order to empower others. This is not to be the praxis of the pious few; the do-gooders; the altruists; the religious zealots. This is ordinary life at its most basic intention. It is also most beautiful. And it is most spiritual.

REFLECTION: *That which is most intrinsic to human existence is also the most profoundly spiritual.*

Renewal

'Renewal does not come *before* mission, but *in* mission.'
Mortimer Arias

Some people are always waiting for the opportune time, for the best setting, the most appropriate opportunity. Some are still waiting. Others are always preparing themselves — more training, more seminars and workshops. Yet some are doing what they never trained themselves for. Others seek to be more spiritual before they embark on anything. So they pray, meditate, fast. But some have come to realise that they *always* need spiritual empowerment. I am not saying that waiting, training and prayer are not important. I am saying that we can over-prepare and never end up doing much. Much of what we need we gain along the way, as we walk the journey of life. We can be empowered in the midst of our doing. And in the rhythm of praxis and reflection, we can learn what no seminar can teach us.

THOUGHT: *Don't wait to be good before you do anything, for you will never be good enough!*

Under threat

'Dry land is the place where human beings can walk with security. The waters of the sea symbolise the horrendous possibilities that menace human beings.'

Rubem Alves

We all experience the dark side of life, that place where we are overwhelmed; powerless; fearful; confused; compromised. These awesome realities may spring from our own wrongdoing. They may also come from evil forces arraigned against us. They may come from the brokenness of our world. But whatever their source, we cannot ignore the shadow side of life. Evil within and without cannot be denied through an overdose of optimism. Here liberal theology has not served us well with its belief in human progress and perfectibility. While much is good in our world, evil is everywhere present in the sanctuary as much as in halls of political power. The threat of darkness need not paralyse us. It can drive us to shelter in God's presence and cause us to resist the powers of our age.

THOUGHT: *In the cross of Christ, evil is exposed and the power of good is brought to the light.*

New eyes

'New experiences of the Spirit are forcing us to look at the old texts with new eyes.'

José Comblin

Openness to the Spirit makes us candidates to receive the renewing power of God. The need for renewal will always remain a constant in our lives. Therefore, renewal should not be sought only in times of crisis, but also in the ebb and flow of our daily existence. For we constantly need to be sustained and empowered by the grace of God. This empowerment by the Spirit can come in many ways: inspiration; creativity; hope; new ways of understanding old texts; new forms of prayer; new ways of outworking our spirituality; new ways of impacting our world. The newness that the Spirit brings is not simply something that hasn't been known before. It is often a bringing back of the old that has fallen into disuse.

MEDITATION: *What new realities has the Spirit brought to your life?*

August

The work for justice and social transformation requires more than pious idealism. It must have a courage that is born of faith and prayer.

Weakness

'There is. . . in us [that] which buckles. . . before temptations to betray our ideals, to surrender integrity and take the path of least resistance.'

Melba Maggay

The work for justice and social transformation requires more than pious idealism. It must have a courage that is born out of faith and prayer. For when the powers of our age are arraigned against us, we easily give way to fear, look for excuses to disengage and embrace the way of compromise. Like Peter, we dare to walk on the water, but we also quickly sink beneath the waves. We make our daring confession of commitment but, in the heat of the moment, we falter in pathetic denial. We shout loud when victory comes our way. But when we are overwhelmed, we readily give way to fear and abandon the cause. We can see, then, that we are no stronger than others, unless we are kept by the grace of God.

PRAYER: *Lord, I am divided between your cause and my safety, your way and my selfishness. Please make me more inwardly whole.* Amen.

Obedience

'There is no ethical decision. . . which does not involve the Christian in a choice between obedience to the divine will and purpose, or infidelity.'

José Míguez Bonino

Unlike the innocent days of childhood, adulthood involves us in an almost never ending set of choices. This does not mean that certain decisions cannot remain firmly in place. The decision to live for God, to be faithful to one's spouse and to serve others does not need to be made anew each day. And yet in one sense, these decisions do need to be reaffirmed. For not only may I be tempted to do otherwise, but other things so easily crowd in and force my central decisions to the periphery. Thus, steps of obedience need to be consolidated. In fact, our commitments need to be made again and again. And all of this is not simply a matter of will power; it is much more being empowered by the grace of God.

THOUGHT: *We can walk various roads. God calls us to walk the narrow way of obedience to his will.*

Togetherness

'Where there's light there's a gathering. Where there are people there's light: a lamp, a fire.'

William, a campesina

While the community of believers and special friendships are important gifts, ordinary human solidarity is a great blessing as well. Gifts of fire, food and hospitality are especially appreciated when one is lost, tired, hungry and soaked to the skin in a rainforest. They are equally appreciated when one enjoys a meal with friends or acquaintances, irrespective of whether the meal is sumptuous or simple; irrespective, too, of whether it is in a beautiful home or in a shanty of the Third World's urban poor. Togetherness, laughter, food, light, acceptance, welcome, openness, trust: these and many other simple virtues make life truly rich for both the giver and the recipient.

REFLECTION: *Hospitality, the gift of open heart and home, can create a simple but truly meaningful solidarity amongst people.*

The power of the dream

'I want questions and not answers. I want the sea and not the harbour.'

Rubem Alves

We have charismatic leaders and administrators; prophets and priests; revolutionaries and bureaucrats; radicals and conservatives; change agents and those committed to the *status quo*. The world obviously needs both. So does the church and every other social institution. We need the spirit of criticism and inquiry as well as that of affirmation. And by temperament and socialisation, many of us will fall into either of these categories. A problem occurs, however, when the bureaucrats take over and the change agents are pushed out. Long term, this is the deathknell of any social institution as well as a particular form of church. Institutions and communities of believers need to be renewed and revitalised. For this, the prophets are needed.

THOUGHT: *Marginalise the change agents and one may well fossilise the church.*

Maturity

'Affective maturity is the capacity to give of oneself
over and above the need to receive.'

Segundo Galilea

The rhythm of the spiritual life is one of receiving
and giving. The one who no longer gives becomes
selfish, bored and satiated. The one who no longer
receives becomes frustrated, driven and burnt out.
The pattern of both giving and receiving is inviol-
able. But this is not to suggest that one becomes the
divine accountant who is always checking to see that
the ledger balances — that, for instance, I will give so
much if I receive what is equivalent. Instead, I am
simply proposing that those who give also need to
receive and that those who receive will need to find
ways to give, including to those who have helped
them. This sets up a rhythm of reciprocity which
makes life full and meaningful for all.

REFLECTION: *Those who are mature have the opportunity to guide, mentor and help others. This is fine,
providing they are also guided, mentored and helped
by others.*

Critique

'We have rarely stopped to ask what critical judgment our faith has to pass on the system.'

Samuel Ryan

Christianity has a long history of supporting the *status quo*, irrespective of whether those in political power perpetrated injustice or not. But the opposite has also been true. Christians and their communities of believers have also been known to resist the powers of this age. In many Third World countries, the church has moved to the side of the poor and has become the champion of the rights of the oppressed. This has resulted in a Christianity with a more prophetic stance and an orientation to social justice. This is good news, for the gospel proclaims liberation from personal sin and structural evil. Not only are the eyes of the blind opened, but those in prison receive their freedom.

REFLECTION: *The church's task is to proclaim the gospel, but also to work for human dignity and justice.*

Discernment

'Only by setting aside the social position committed
to the dominant ideology will it be possible for us to
realise the prerequisite for an act of discernment.'

L.B. Libanio

Those in power would have everyone else
believe that what they do is ultimately for
everyone's benefit. But the ideological justification by the elite is often nothing else than self-
justification. Those who are the disadvantaged in
a society must learn to resist these powerful
ideologies. And the place to start is to accept that
God does not will poverty, oppression and injustice.
If these realities are a people's experience, then it
is important that they know that God is committed
to changing such circumstances. This move
beyond passivity and resignation opens the door
of hope and makes possible the long journey
towards justice.

MEDITATION: *The most powerful genesis in the
change process is to believe that things can and should
be different and to begin to work accordingly.*

The grace of God

'I don't think there is anyone who needs God's help and grace as much as I do.'

Mother Teresa

Some claim that it all gets easier. The longer we are Christians, the more settled and stronger we become. Growth in maturity means that a life of faith and obedience becomes almost second nature. While there is some truth in this, it is basically a wrong understanding of the Christian journey. The Christian life requires ongoing commitment. It requires new empowerment by the Holy Spirit. It is sustained by the grace of God which needs constantly to impact on our lives. While our later struggles may not be the same as those which characterised the beginnings of our Christian journey, we need the grace of God in word, sacrament and community throughout the whole of our journey of faith.

PRAYER: *Lord, when I become sure and confident in my discipleship, give me the humility to rediscover how much I really need you.* Amen!

The Spirit

'The experience of the Spirit launches men and women out into the world as though imbued with superhuman energy to tackle superhuman tasks.'

José Comblin

People can make all sorts of claims that what they are saying and doing is the result of the guidance and power of the Spirit. Strange cults and communitarian experiments have sprung up this way. The work of the Spirit, however, needs careful discernment. One sign of the Spirit is magnifying Christ. The Spirit always draws us into the life of Jesus. A second sign has to do with mission. The Spirit empowers people to speak God's word with boldness and to perform miracles in the name of Jesus. People with the Spirit are not selfish and inward focussed. They are driven from the upper room, the place of retreat, into the marketplace to proclaim good news.

PRAYER: *Lord, my faith is often so small. Help me not to do your work in my own strength, but to rely on you and your power. Amen.*

Commitment

'The initial response the proclamation of the reign [of God] produces. . . is one of joy and happiness. Later there will be a call to live up to the values of the coming reign.'

Juan Ramón Moreno

The genesis of the Christian life is not service. Nor is the genius of Christianity that it is a credit religion where one earns points on the right side of the ledger through all sorts of worthwhile activities. Being a Christian has a profoundly different orientation. It begins and ends with a miracle — the grace of God which touches us in our confusion, alienation and sin and brings us peace and forgiveness. This is a recurring miracle which sustains us in our life journey. And out of this miracle we live a life of gratitude and service expressing our thanks to the God who has been so merciful to us.

REFLECTION: *The movement of the Christian life is always from grace to obedience, gratitude to service, receiving to giving and celebration to sacrifice.*

Reflection

'A higher level of reflection on my existence and the factors conditioning it will enable me to grasp things in the Word of God that a more superficial and inauthentic way of life would not notice.'

Juan Luis Segundo

What God is saying to us can come to us as flashes of light. This is revelation. It can also come to us in other ways. Reflection is one way. But this is more than simply a meditative reading of scripture. It involves the bringing together of two horizons — the horizon of my social existence and the horizon of the Bible. When I reflect on my dark side — the enigma of life, the pain of injustice and the brokenness in our social order and bring these issues and concerns to scripture — I can hear things from the Bible that I would not have heard had I not asked these questions. When we press the Bible with our deeper questions seeking God's wisdom, we will receive answers that we had not anticipated.

THOUGHT: *The more we are willing to face the reality of our existence, the more we can come to God, seeking answers.*

In the school of hard knocks

'The very challenge of the world can be the sandpaper to polish the sanctity of those who seek to become perfect disciples of Christ in the lay life.'

Thomas H. Green

There are no short cuts in the journey to maturity. Whether one joins a religious order or one remains a lay person, the journey of discipleship is similar. It involves not only our surrender to God in faith and obedience, but also submitting to God's purpose for our life. More particularly, it has to do with God forming and shaping us in the midst of life's struggles and contradictions. God can use the many and varied circumstances of our life to make us vessels of honour and instruments of blessing. Therefore, let us not run away from the difficult circumstances of life nor waste our sorrows. Instead, let us trust the God of all grace to use all things to make us fit for his use.

REFLECTION: *To be shaped by God's hand of blessing is one thing. To be shaped by the difficulties of life is a blessing that we seldom recognise.*

The seed of faith

'It . . . seems to me that the word of God is tiny and insignificant because it sprouts in our hearts and you almost can't see it. But then I tell it to someone else, and so it grows and spreads like a great tree, and this tree is the transformation of the world.'

Manuel, a campesino

It is amazing what a word of hope, act of love, prayer of faith can achieve. The power of these activities, however, does not reside in the virtue of the actor or the faith of the recipient, although these factors are never irrelevant. Instead, power lies in the accompanying grace of God. It is God who makes our prayers and service effective. God lights the torch and fans the flame. God turns darkness to light and despair into hope. This does not mean that we do not play a part. It simply means that without the power of God's Spirit, nothing very much changes despite all of our efforts.

PRAYER: *Lord, may the little or much that I do be done in love; and, in doing it, may I look to you for your empowerment.* Amen.

Lord of all

'Jesus Christ. . . is not only the Lord of small places
like the heart, the soul, the church; he is the cosmic
Lord of large spaces like politics.'

Leonardo Boff

Jesus, Son of God and Man of peace, reconciler
and healer, Lord and friend, seeks to live in both
the broken and the whole places of our lives. He
has grace for both the innocent child and the
cynical adult. There is the blessing of forgiveness
as well as that of creativity. There is wisdom for
prayer as well as politics. Jesus not only has
relevance for an interior spirituality. His word
and actions also pave the way for social transformation. Jesus is, therefore, as much at home in
the marketplace as the sanctuary. And it is not a
matter of bringing him into either sphere. He is
already there and needs only to be found with
the eye of faith.

MEDITATION: *Lord, in these reflective moments, I
want to open to you both some of the hurting places of
my life and the places where I am strong and confident.*

Transformation

'The spiritual life must be efficacious for the transformation of the secular reality around us.'
Jon Sobrino

Why bother when so much is broken in our world and nothing seems to improve in an ultimate way? Why pray and work when human selfishness and the powers of the dark world negate so much that is good? The answer to these difficult questions is both simple and profound. The light has shone in our darkness. Christ broke the chains of death. Reconciliation between us and God is now a marvellous possibility. Grace is freely extended. Therefore, change is amongst us and transformation is an exciting possibility. Being changed ourselves, we cannot but become the agents of change. Touched by the grace of God, we cannot but proclaim good news to others. And, empowered by the Spirit, we cannot but be thrust into the world, working for its transformation.

REFLECTION: *When we are truly changed and concerned for others, we carry with us new life for them.*

Concern

'Without love, sympathy and concern for the
people, liberating work is not possible.'

Clodovis Boff

Sometimes we make false contrasts. We suggest
that love is sloppy sentimentalism, while the
work of justice arises out of passionate concern
and analysis. Yet nothing is further from the
truth. Love can serve the cause of justice. Those
whom we love, we should also identify with and
draw close to in order to hear their heart-cry and
concerns. Those whom we love, we should care
for and work on their behalf, seeking to bring
about changes that will benefit them. The work
of transformation, therefore, is not simply one of
strategies and programs. It also has to do with a
love that stays long enough to listen, to identify
with and to journey with those who suffer injustice and marginalisation.

THOUGHT: *Anger cannot work the righteousness of
God. Only love can inspire us to work for change in
both the oppressor and the oppressed.*

Perseverance

'Lord, help those who are always beginning anew
on the way of holiness, to persevere.'
                                        Dom Helder Camara

The progress of the Christian life is not necessarily like a steady climb from the foothills to the
mountain top. It has much more to do with
sometimes ending up in a gully that leads
nowhere, necessitating that we retrace our steps
and start anew. Sometimes, it may even be like
being swept off the mountain face by an
avalanche, resulting in the need to find new
courage to recommence the journey. While the
Christian journey is difficult for all, it is especially
difficult for those who live with hurts from the
past and live in difficult circumstances — those
in dysfunctional families; unworkable marriages;
economic poverty; and workplaces of injustice.

MEDITATION: *Identify an area in your life where
you are struggling and where you need to find grace
in order to persevere.*

Social justice

'The Christian church has yet to learn and practise
and teach that Christian love is more than charity; it
is social justice.'

Geevarghese Mar Osthathios

Charity will always be called for. There are always emergencies that require the quick response
of love and concern. But there are many groups
of people and communities that require more
than charity. They need justice. It is possible that
the continual giving of charity to such groups
can become an act of injustice. Charity can be the
avoidance mechanism taking us away from the
harder work of justice, which seeks not only to
provide immediate care, but to restore people's
dignity, economic viability and the opportunity
for self-determination.

REFLECTION: *While charity may well involve
sacrificial giving, the work of justice involves the long
journey of social transformation.*

Movement

'Jesus carefully built a large following which was not just another religious sect, but was an alternative centre of power in Israel.'

Vishal Mangalwadi

Jesus responded to individuals and brought forgiveness, healing and hope to their lives. Jesus mobilised men and women for ministry. These were part of his apostolic band. These were given special training and the task to proclaim the kingdom of God. But Jesus' vision was much wider than this. He sought to make an impact on the whole nation of Israel, but gained a following particularly among the poor. Crowds came to him and he saw them as sheep without a shepherd. His compassion and concern for them meant that he not only wanted to bless them, but to guide them into true worship and a commitment to the kingdom of God.

THOUGHT: *The power structures that Jesus sought to create were not those of institutions and organisations, but of people set free to love and worship God and their neighbour.*

Empowerment

'Empowerment is drawing out the gifts that lie in people and helping those gifts to flourish.'

Priscilla Padolina

It is sheer arrogance to assume that the people we are helping have nothing and that we have to contribute everything to their well-being. Even the poorest have something to give. They have their wisdom gained from a long journey of struggle and pain and they have developed remarkable coping mechanisms and survival skills. These they can contribute along with their sense of hope and quiet dignity. True empowerment, therefore, starts where people are and maximises what they can contribute. It assumes that people have gifts, skills and resources. At the same time, it seeks to tap the hidden potential in people and their communities. This means that those who come to help must first be listeners, befrienders and mobilisers and enablers, rather than those who know everything and have everything.

Deuteronomy 6: 20–25　　　　　**August 21**

Redeeming the past

'Memory does not preserve the past as something over and done with, but as a living force which moves the present on toward the future.'

Carlos Mesters

The past is not a rocket capsule that we simply jettison on our journey to the future. The past is woven into the very fabric of our being, for both good or ill. While the good of the past can produce stability, security and a sense of well-being, the good can also produce indolence and self-satisfaction. And while the bad can produce anger, bitterness, hurt and dys-functionality, the opposite can also take place. The intended evil has worked for our good.

As a result, we come away stronger and more resilient. The critical factor in the mixed bag of blessings that comes our way has to do with how we process both the good and the ill. If we don't waste our sorrows and are truly thankful for the blessings, then we have a rich heritage with which to move towards the future.

MEDITATION: *Identify some key blessings which have remained beneficial and some key difficulties which have empowered your life.*

John 15: 5–8   **August 22**

Praxis

'Accepting the word and making it life and concrete deed is the point of departure for an understanding of the faith.'   *Gustavo Gutiérrez*

The Word made flesh is the heart of the mystery of Christianity. It represents the move of God from the realm of the obscure to the most concrete. In the incarnation, the birth of Jesus, the invisibility of God becomes most visible. There should be a similar momentum in the realm of faith. The inner transformative work of the Spirit, when the word of hope takes root in one's life, results in outward changes. Slowly but surely, one's values, outlook and priorities begin to change. Old concerns are replaced with a new desire to follow and serve Christ. And a passion for the kingdom of God becomes the central thrust of one's existence. All of this is also the move from inner values to outward expression; from an interior spirituality to an outward sociality; from faith to deed; from prayer to action; from inner desire to concrete expression.

PRAYER: *Lord, may my interior world be rich in the resources of your kingdom and may that richness be expressed in the way I live my whole life.* Amen.

Transforming prayer

'Let him draw us to something new, to a more transforming and less consoling prayer — prayer that is more like surgery than like a birthday party.'

Thomas H. Green

There are many different moments of prayer. So prayer takes differing forms. Much prayer has to do with meeting our needs. But there is also the prayer of worship and adoration. Here, our concerns are not in focus, but the honour and greatness of God predominates. Another important form of prayer is seeking God's sheltering presence. It's the prayer of intimacy; closeness; comfort. It comes out of a sense of weakness or vulnerability. But some of the tougher forms of prayer have to do with relinquishment and transformation. While relinquishment has to do with an abandonment to do the will of God, transformation embraces the difficult process of change and renewal. Here, we are aware not only of our weaknesses and failures, but also of persistent problems that need surgery and healing.

REFLECTION: *To be in touch with our shadow side need not be a morbid introspection, but the beginning of the journey on the road to change.*

Beyond fear

'I believe that the two things work together, loving and not being afraid. The more you love, the more you get rid of fear.'

William, a campesino

While a fear of failure may spur us on to greater effort, many fears have the opposite effect. They immobilise us. We see the giants of difficulty on the road and, in fear, we take sidetracks – or, worse, we become and remain paralysed. While certain fears are like well placed warning signs along the road, others are shadowy spectres of behemoth proportion, but of little substance. These deflect us from the way we should take. These fears cannot be welcomed, let alone entertained, but must be ardently resisted. And we should particularly resist fears that spring from the nether world which deflect us from walking in the ways and purposes of God. Here, we are challenged not to give way to the spirit of fear, but to trust that God will carry us over the abyss to the place of safety.

REFLECTION: *Fear is the great temptation that leaves us where we are when we should be moving forward.*

Against hope

'Successes and failures are two sides of the same temptation against hope.'

Segundo Galilea

To hope is to choose life, to embrace the future, to be open to new possibilities. Hope is so much more than the antidote to cynicism and despair. Hope is the fuel that keeps us going in the face of difficulties and propels us to look and work for solutions in the face of great odds. To be without hope is to embrace death. The gift and blessing of hope, however, is always under threat. Not only can repeated failure undermine hope, but an arrogant sense of achievement can lull us into the false attitude that there is nothing left to hope for. But the greater threat to hope is the loss of faith in the God who welcomes us into the future and a loss of freedom where options and choices are no longer available to us.

REFLECTION: *As long as hope continues to flicker, however dimly, in the human heart, the surge toward life will continue.*

Taking responsibility

'To study a situation is indissolubly linked with accepting the burden of that situation and becoming responsible for the situation.'

Ignacio Ellacuría

There are people who have an insatiable hunger for knowledge. They observe, read, reflect, integrate. Their desire to know more has no bounds. This quest for knowledge is commendable. But knowledge can never simply be for the satisfaction of our curiosity, for we are part of the human community. And in that community we have to play our part. There we can use our gifts, use our resources and make our contribution toward the greater good. Thus, knowledge always brings with it responsibility. And the more we know, the more responsible we become. The desire to know, therefore, needs to be complemented by the willingness to act. This is not to suggest that we can do everything and that our doing will always have the desired outcomes. But not to act is an act of cowardice.

REFLECTION: *There is a powerful cycle of contact, exposure, information gathering, analysis and reflection which then leads to practical involvement through empowering, strategising, mobilising and implementation.*

Inner and outer worlds

'The struggle between sin and salvation is not con-
fined to some inner world. . . it is fought out in the
economic and political and in the cultural and ecclesiastical spheres as well.'

Donal Dorr

God's transformative grace makes its initial impact
in the mind and heart of the person. We are changed
within. We become spiritually alive and at peace
with God. Things do not stop there. God's grace is
for every aspect of our lives: not just the personal,
but also the social; not just the individual, but also
the familial; not just the spiritual, but also the
economic; not just the religious, but also the secular;
not just the recreational, but also the workaday
world. Not only is there grace for every aspect of our
lives, but everywhere there are challenges for us to
pray and work for the kingdom of God. The clergy
person and the lawyer, the economist and the poet,
the prophet and the politician are all called to serve
God and to resist the forces of evil.

THOUGHT: *In our thinking and our loving, in our
creating and our caring, in our building and our
forming, we are called to manifest the grace of God.*

Hope and transformation

'We have gone from an experience of oppression, marginalisation and suffering, to a realm of hope that is impelling us toward change.'

Luz Beatriz Arellano

Difficulties can lead to resignation and despair. It is possible to feel so overwhelmed that one gives up. The struggle ceases; hope is gone. But the opposite is also a possibility and is, in fact, what is happening among the poor in many Third World countries. Difficulties and oppression have produced a strength and determination not only to survive, but to work for change and social transformation. The base ecclesial communities are but one manifestation of this impulse. What is encouraging in these developments is that the church has moved to the side of the poor and is using its personnel and resources to empower the poor. This does not mean that the church is simply blessing the poor, but that it is renewing its own life by becoming a church from below.

MEDITATION: *Identify how difficulties have produced strength and fortitude in your life.*

Breaking the bonds

'Freedom begins when the inner shackles of fear are broken. All liberation must be first spiritual and internal.'

Miguel D'Escoto

True freedom must ultimately express itself in changed institutions and communities and in changed laws. In other words, freedom must become a structured reality. But the impulse towards freedom usually begins somewhere else. While the movement towards liberation can originate with the powerful in a society, it more frequently begins with those at the margins. And for such, freedom begins as a dream, in the visioning of a better world. This belief in new possibilities can have spiritual origins. From the idea that all people are made in God's image, that God sends rain and blessing upon all and that God is passionate about justice can spring the vision that things can and should be different in our social world.

THOUGHT: *God hates oppression and therefore loves justice. As a consequence, God will empower and journey with those who seek liberation.*

Community

"To live sharing everything, from the knowledge of God to a practical sympathy with the sufferings of others, to holding material goods in common, is a life-affirming alternative.'

Juan Hernández Pico

The practice of human solidarity or community continues to be one of the dangerous memories of early Christianity. While this challenging ideal resonates much more readily with peoples of the Third World, it continues to be an embarrassment to those living in the First World. There, an isolating and self-sufficient individualism continues to be the cultural ideal. Fortunately, there are exceptions — monasticism, the Brethren of the Common Life, the Anabaptists, the Moravians and, into our present era, the communities of Catholic charismatic renewal and the house churches of Protestantism. These, as well as the base ecclesial communities of the Third World, act as signposts that the Christian life involves love of God and a community of sharing and service to our neighbour, including our enemies.

THOUGHT: *To build community is to practice justice.*

Sounds of silence

'Our experience in Negros [in the Philippines] shows that the silence of priests and teachers is necessary if Negros is to be kept a land of plantations with obedient, subservient. . . and silent workers who believe they can do nothing.'

Niall O'Brien

The ultimate form of 'depowerment' is to accept the way things are and to believe that significant changes are not possible. The powerful have always tried to make those who are less fortunate believe that some are meant to rule while others are meant to be subservient. The power of this ideology is not easily broken. But it can occur when the poor learn that destiny is also in their hands, that ideologies can be demasked, that oppression is a curse that needs to be overturned and that the poor can and do make their contribution to national wellbeing. To facilitate this development, the poor need those who will journey with them, empower them and advocate on their behalf.

THOUGHT: *Silence is usually acquiescence. It should become a powerful form of protest.*

September

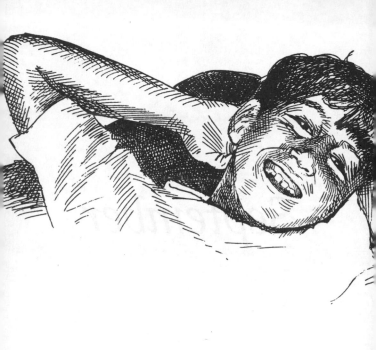

God himself offers us the gift of friendship.

Courageous

'If we are to have the strength to stand steadfast in persecution and to be of support to those who work with us or depend on us, we shall need a special spirit of fortitude, a strength of spirit that will be mightier than our fears and terrors.'

Jon Sobrino

When it comes to God's call, we are often deaf. When it comes to God's demand, we are often unavailable. When we are challenged to give our all, we often hold back. When sacrifices are asked of us, we often have excuses. And when we need to stand firm against the evil one and the powers of this age, we are often fearful or compromising. Whenever these things are not true of us, then the grace of God is especially with us. Then God has poured his love upon us and we are strong, despite our frailties and our fears.

REFLECTION: *When we are weak we can be strong, but only as we look to the Lord who is our rock.*

Friendship

'Time is precious, but friendship is not cheap. When we give of our time, we give ourselves.'

Isabelo Magalit

God himself offers us the gift of friendship. This involves both his love for us and his commitment to us. We also receive the blessing of friendship through our immediate and wider family. But surprisingly, there is more. There are also special people with whom we have a sense of affinity and whom we have learnt to trust and come close to. These are the special ones with whom we have journeyed part of our life. These are the ones who have encouraged us, to whom we have turned for help and advice and who have made special room in their hearts and lives for us. And when we, in turn, have also been able to bless and challenge them, then how rich we are with this special gift!

MEDITATION: *Reflect on what your special friends have contributed to your life and think of ways you can bless them.*

Indifference

'Making ourselves indifferent does not mean putting an end to all desire, but transferring our desire. . . to that which appears. . . to be most conducive.'

Juan Luis Segundo

The classic writers on spirituality, including St Ignatius of Loyola, all speak of the gift of indif ference. This does not mean that we become numb and unconcerned regarding the things around us. It means, basically, that we do not use anything which, while good in itself, may take us away from the primary purpose of our existence: to love, worship and serve the God who has redeemed us. This approach to life does not say that good things are bad. It simply says that sometimes good things need to be left to one side. It means that for the sake of the higher good, some things may need to be relinquished.

THOUGHT: *To say 'no' to what is good is never foolish if the good would deter us from our purpose or would possess us in inappropriate ways.*

Gathered and scattered

'The church gathers in order to scatter; it withdraws inwardly only to better serve the world outwardly.'

Melba Maggay

We need to be nurtured. Therefore, we need to draw close to God, be in touch with ourselves and in fellowship with the community of believers. When the church gathers together, this should never be simply for meetings, but for worship, teaching and nurture. And to be nurtured involves coming in touch with our needs, sharing those needs with God and others and receiving the input, encouragement and healing that we are seeking. Thus empowered, we have perseverance for the journey, courage for the difficulties, faith and hope for the insurmountable problems, patience for the unexpected. Being nurtured, we can share and serve because we have been graced by the abundant love of God.

REFLECTION: *Withdrawal for refreshment and renewal is not incidental to our service, but central.*

The seed of sacrifice

'Despite — or thanks to — the immense price that is being paid, the present situation is nourishing new life.'

Gustavo Gutiérrez

While in the First World the gospel of an easy believism continues to be preached, in the Third World things are vastly different. There, the church can point to its martyrs who have been faithful even unto death. Rather than these awful realities diminishing the power and witness of the church, the opposite is taking place. The blood of the martyrs is the seed of the church. Men and women who previously despised the church because of its compromise with the powers of this age, now stumble into the sanctuary and bow the knee to the God who has poured out his Spirit upon his people.

REFLECTION: *Great men and women are formed when great sacrifices are made.*

A heart of mercy

'The good news exists simply because God is a God with a heart of mercy.'

Juan Ramón Moreno

Sadly, some people see God as vengeful, demanding and authoritarian. They have never experienced God's embrace, gentleness, forgiveness and mercy. Maybe their experience of parental figures or other people in positions of leadership has caused them to view God in the light of their own unhappy experiences. Others may have experienced a legalistic form of Christianity or authoritarian clergy. But while God is never condoning or lackadaisical with regard to evil, he is merciful to those who turn to him in repentance and faith. The gospel trumpets the good news that our failure and sin need not be the last word. God's grace can triumph over the greatest evil.

PRAYER: *Lord, help me never to shut you out of my failure, weakness and sin. Help me to run to you in faith and repentance.* Amen.

The body of Christ

'They killed that body, but it goes on living, giving life to the world, and all who live for others are also part of that body, are bread that gives life to the world.'

Gerardo, a campesina

Jesus Christ is with us in many ways. He is present in and through the Holy Spirit. He is there as the Living Word in the preached word. He is present as sacrament, bringing forgiveness and cleansing. And he is present in the community of believers and in the individuals who comprise that community. Thus, we celebrate that Jesus is alive and amongst us! We carry him in our hearts and worship him in our midst. And he carries us into our neighbourhoods, places of work and even to the farthest parts of the globe. Carrying Jesus and being carried by him means that we point to him as the source of life and that we serve others and the world as part of our witness.

MEDITATION: *How is Christ nourishing you? And how are you nourishing others?*

Working together

'Working with people is an art. . . and art is learnt in
the process of doing.'

Clodovis Boff

There is nothing immediately beneficial about
participatory processes. Such processes tend to
be slow and cumbersome. It is, therefore, much
quicker to make use of the expert and the leader,
to make decisions for people and to set things in
motion so that goals and objectives can be
achieved. To use consensus-building processes
seems to get things off to a slow start. But in the
long run, this may be the better way to go. For if
people can learn to discuss things, to listen to
each other and to discern what needs to be done,
then they are on the way to being empowered. If
they can also agree to work cooperatively and to
share resources in order to execute their plans,
then they are learning the art of working
together.

THOUGHT: *The more people can do together and for
each other, the more they build community.*

The Holy Spirit

'In the Bible, the role of the Spirit is found in activities more usually associated with maternity and femininity. . . inspiring, helping, enveloping, bringing to birth.'

José Comblin

In spite of the growing secularisation of our age and an increasing rationalistic approach to life, the growth of Pentecostal and charismatic churches continues. This may well reflect the continuing hunger of the human spirit for the transcendental. While the Word is important in the community of believers, the Spirit is equally significant. In fact, the Spirit makes the Word alive, present and relevant. Furthermore, the Spirit brings Jesus the Living Word close to us. And finally, the Spirit beautifies, empowers and guides us. The Spirit comforts, anoints and carries us along as a sailboat catches the wind.

REFLECTION: *With the Spirit, rigid structures are shattered and new life comes as the breeze.*

Co-worker

'Man is a co-worker. . . [and] has to be in the world,
involved with the activities of the world — immersed
in apostolic action and service, engaged in the constant
seeking, finding and doing of God's will.'

Ramon Bautista

God empowers us with different abilities and
gifts. Some have the gift of a critical mind. Others
have the gift of mercy and care. Some become
scientists. Others make medical care or social
work their vocation. Some become artists.
Others become clergy. And while some people
have the gift of imagining new possibilities,
others are good at organising and mobilising
people to get the job done and others are good at
maintaining the systems that have been created.
Whatever our gift and vocation, we are called to
use them to glorify God, build up the community
of believers and transform our world.

MEDITATION: *What are my gifts? Does my vocation
allow me to use my gifts? How am I using my gifts?*

Blessings in tough times

'Most of us take the Lord for granted in good times and are only brought to our knees in hard times.'
Thomas H. Green

There is a particular gift in the blessing of good times. It is the easy rhythm of life and the happiness of abundant provision. This makes for carefree living and the joy of celebration. The danger, of course, is that we take things for granted, fail to be thankful and grumble in the midst of good times. There is also a special gift in the blessing of tough times. This is learning to have courage and patience and to persevere in the face of all odds. Here one learns to trust the God of the silences and the dark night of the soul. Here, too, lurks danger, for one can feel abandoned and overwhelmed — or, worse, one can become bitter in times of difficulty. We do not need to seek the one blessing or the other. They will come our way. But we do need to seek God's grace in each blessing.

THOUGHT: *It is not so much what comes our way, but what we do with blessing or difficulty.*

True riches

'There is but one richness: participation in your [God's] life, your divinity, your creative power, your will. Other riches are false riches, piled up in selfishness.'

Dom Helder Camara

In our very materialistic world, many do not see riches in terms of virtue, character and integrity. Not only do they not see riches in terms of inward qualities: they don't see them as spiritual qualities, either. A person of faith and prayer can still be hungry and can still be oppressed, some are quick to point out. And those who are cynical, fondly remind us that to wait for riches in heaven is simply to give up your slice of the pie here on earth. But the contrast is false which suggests that to serve self and the devil means material blessings here and to serve God results only in spiritual blessings in the hereafter. The issue is: serve God whether you have little and much; for, in a life of obedience, true joy and happiness is found.

REFLECTION: *The life of obedience is being with God and working together with God. Thus, it is a life of presence and partnership. In this, a person is truly blessed.*

Truth

'Theology rediscovers the subversive and dangerous memory of Jesus of Nazareth who, while among us, did not say, I am tradition, but rather, I am the truth.'

Leonardo Boff

Early Christianity has many dangerous memories. The defeated are victorious, since Jesus rose from the dead after the shameful cross. Sinners are welcomed, but the religious are excluded, since Jesus came not for those who had it all together, but for the broken and the humble. The great are the weak, since God the father of the poor is able to come to those who recognise their need and look to him for salvation and liberation. The list could go on, for in early Christianity we see the upside-down values of the kingdom of God where the poor are blessed and the rich are sent away empty-handed.

REFLECTION: *In our churches and in our personal faith, have we so domesticated Jesus that he simply affirms our values and traditions? Or is Jesus still the radical who turns our world upside down?*

Love of our neighbour

'We are not asked to love the neighbour as neighbour, but as ourselves.'

Geevarghese Mar Osthathios

Anyone is my neighbour to whom I make myself present or who becomes present to me. Being present involves presence, and presence means that I make myself open and vulnerable to the other person. What happens from that point onwards is open to an infinite array of possibilities. A neighbour may become an enemy. A neighbour may also become a friend. And a friend may become a partner for life. Initially, a neighbour can only be an acquaintance. But who knows what may develop? Therefore, in the act of loving our neighbour we may gain a friend for ever.

REFLECTION: *Every acquaintance is a candidate for true friendship. And when friendship emerges, we realise how great a gift we have received.*

Full humanity

'God was at work through the servant ministry and lifestyle of Jesus, taking the side of the poor and the victims of current injustices to enable them to achieve full humanity.'

Vinay Samuel

Receiving the grace of the forgiveness of sins does not mean that all our present problems are solved; all our past hurts healed; our personality difficulties overcome; our relational problems solved; our intellectual difficulties regarding the life of faith answered; and our social and economic difficulties rectified. If that were the case, then coming to faith would be pure magic. Instead, we are called to a life of discipleship where Jesus by his Spirit promises to journey with us and we journey together with the community of believers. In this way, we can grow and experience the fullness of life God has promised to those who belong to him.

REFLECTION: *Wholeness does not come with conversion. But conversion is an important part of one's growth into wholeness.*

New order

'This new order would be made visible in the community of his own disciples, the firstfruits of a new humanity marked by love to God and neighbour as well as renunciation of personal prestige, material wealth and earthly power.'

C. René Padilla

The Christian community has such potential for discipling and caring for its own and making an impact in our tired and broken world. But this potential will never be realised if the community of believers seeks to be a mere repetition of what is already happening in our world. If the community can do the opposite and walk in the footsteps of her Master, then its mission can be effective. Living by the divine contrariness of Jesus; practising the values of the upside-down kingdom; sharing faith and resources; welcoming the marginalised; sharing power; living authentically; and challenging the powers of this age: the contemporary community of believers can be an insertion in the world that will keep the dream of the kingdom of God alive.

THOUGHT: *The key motif of the kingdom of God is premised on the life of the Suffering Servant.*

The Spirit's power

'The coming of the Spirit upon the disciples not only signals the arrival of a new era. . . it also speaks of the disciples' empowerment for effective witness.'
Nelson Estrada

Some segments of the worldwide Christian communion wish to play off against each other the power of the Word and that of the Spirit. The Word without the Spirit can lead to a dead orthodoxy. The Spirit without the Word can lead to libertinism. Both extremes should be avoided. But that the Spirit's work is essential is without doubt. The Spirit makes us alive in Christ. The Spirit empowers us for service. The Spirit enlightens us and directs us in our praying. The Spirit endows us with gifts and shapes our life with virtues. But the Spirit also builds and guides the community of believers and sustains the created order.

MEDITATION: *Gentle as a dove; penetrating like oil; purifying like fire; giving birth; empowering: think about the way the Spirit needs to work in you.*

The power of solidarity

'When we're isolated we don't communicate the message of the gospel, which is a message of unity, of brotherhood. We brothers and sisters have to form a community of love.'

Olivia, a campesina

So much of the emphasis on evangelism is cast in individualistic terms. It is one person sharing the faith with another. While this is an important reality, it is not the whole story. Sharing the good news can also occur communally. There is nothing quite so powerful as people having the opportunity to see Christianity in action in communities or in small groups. Here is where faith and life meet. Here, Bible and world meet. Here, certainty as well as doubt can be expressed. Here, needs as well as victories can be acknowledged. To see something of the Christian life in action is a wonderful way in which to learn the gospel. This is not to say that people's experience should be equated with the gospel; but it is a challenge to see the gospel fleshed out in human reality.

THOUGHT: *A community which is welcoming and open to the world can make a great impact.*

The suffering Christ

'Christ is hidden under the suffering appearance of anyone who is hungry, anyone who is naked, anyone who is homeless or dying.'

Mother Teresa

There may be nothing particularly religious about some people among the poor. They, too, have their share of misfits and troublemakers. But whether religious or not, well-integrated or not, the poor always confront us with a particular kind of challenge. Theirs is the suppressed or overt cry for justice and compassion. And embedded in that cry is the covert challenge of Jesus that confronts our rationalisations and complacency. That silent voice calls us to compassion and care. And sometimes, much more deeply, it calls us to a life of serving with the poor. While the rich pose no challenge of this kind, they, like the poor, are equally in need of the grace of God.

REFLECTION: *The poor never cease to evangelise us with the gospel to care for those who are the least.*

Suffering humanity

'We have the capacity to feed ourselves several times over, but we are daily haunted by the spectacle of the gaunt dregs of humanity shuffling along in endless queues, with bowls to collect what the charity of the world has provided.'

Desmond Tutu

There are the millions in our world who live with daily hunger, frequent sickness and meaningless employment as street vendors or scavengers at our city's rubbish dumps. These have hardly ever graced school with their presence and live with dogged perseverance the cycle of existence which knows little joy and silent despair. These are the ones which our world does not know. From these we have turned our faces. And in our abandonment of them, we further scar the image of God in their lives and condemn the quality and virtue of our own humanity.

REFLECTION: *We live between the times — between the coming of Jesus in humility and his rulership at the end of the age. Across that seemingly endless span of time echo and re-echo the haunting and ethereal words: 'As you have done it to the least of these. . .'*

Social change

'Integral to the proclamation of the gospel of the kingdom is the proclamation of hope for social justice through social change.'

Tito Paredes

The good news of the gospel is that, through Christ, we come into a living relationship with God. But there is more good news. We also come into new relationships with others. The new vertical relationship spills over onto the horizontal level. New social relationships become the sign for new possibilities in our broken world. When enmity is broken down between classes of people or ethnic groups; when men and women can work in equality and partnership; when justice is done and the poor are empowered; when strategies for peacemaking are used instead of those which oppress and alienate — then, in a small way, a new world is being born.

THOUGHT: *If the church can continue to be a reconciled and a reconciling community of believers, then new energies that celebrate life can be diffused into the world.*

Prophetic church

'The tensions between. . . institutional church and prophetic church seem to be unavoidable.'

Francisco Dardichon

That the church should have two faces should be welcomed. But I am not talking about the divine and human. There is nothing divine about the church. Divinity belongs to God alone. The church is a profoundly human institution which partakes of the grace and love of God, but never has this as its own possession. The church only has what it has received from God; otherwise it has little. But when the church lives under the benediction of God and in faithfulness to his word, the church has much to give. The tension in the church lies in its being faithful to God rather than relying on its own institutional power. Here, the prophetic church poses a continual challenge to the church as institution. The prophetic church means the faithful church — faithful to Jesus and the Spirit.

THOUGHT: *Every institution needs ongoing renewal. So does the church.*

Evangelism

'True evangelism is *incarnate*: proclamation in
words and deeds in a concrete situation.'

*Statement of the Evangelical
Methodist Church in Bolivia*

Word and deed belong together in a symbiotic
relationship. Spoken love must issue in deeds of
love. But deeds of love may well be accompanied
by an explanatory: 'I love you.' Words explain
deeds. But equally, deeds exemplify words. This
by no means exhausts all that could be said. Not
only may the word inspire, direct and facilitate
the deed, but the deed may also create the word.
What I mean by this is that sometimes our action
in the world is particularly creative and when it
is, we need to find new ways of explaining what
has happened.

REFLECTION: *In Jesus, we see word and deed combined in such a way that they become an explosive
force for good in our world.*

Seed

'Jesus sowed his seed in our hearts, then off he went. . . He knew things would not be ideal. There were the birds and the droughts, the weeds and the insects, the parasites and the blights. But there was also the power of the seed itself.'
Joseph G. Donders

As human beings, we are 'thrown' into the world. It is our habitat. The world sustains us and we are called to shape it and be its caretakers. This 'throwness' is also our lot as women and men of faith. We are called to live the Genesis mandate in being vice-regents under God, as well as seeking to be part of God's redemptive purposes in our world. None of this suggests that the world is simply a welcome place. We also experience its difficulty, its refractory nature and its violence and pain. This is true both of the natural world and the social world. But in this world we need not be afraid. We are not abandoned orphans. We are graced by God and carry within us the seed of the kingdom which both sustains and empowers us.

THOUGHT: *We are scattered like seed in the most unlikely places. May we bear good fruit there!*

Structural evil

'Social sin [is] the crystallisation. . . of individuals'
sins into permanent structures that keeps sin in
being and makes its force to be felt by the majority
of people.'

Oscar Romero

Lots of specific examples immediately spring to
mind when we think about the reality of structural evil: political oppression on the part of a
military dictatorship; unjust wages which keep a
major segment of a population in relative poverty;
institutions such as hospitals or schools which
were meant to serve all and now serve only the
elite. But structural evil can also come much
closer to home. When abusive patterns exist within
a family network, structural evil has found a home.
And when the church excludes the meaningful and
leadership participation of women, then evil has also
penetrated into the sanctuary.

REFLECTION: *Understanding, confronting and deal-
ing with structural evil requires comprehensive
strategies and is not simply the domain of the sole
crusader for righteousness.*

The power of the gospel

'The power of the gospel. . . creates solidarity and
fraternity; it causes the emergence and growth of
courage and hope.'

Alvaro Barreiro

The gospel is good news for many people. It is bad
news for some. It is good news for the needy, the
poor and the hopeless. But it is bad news for those
who think that they already have everything and
therefore have no need of God's forgiveness,
friendship and empowerment. But whenever the
gospel finds a lodging place in the heart of individuals and in an entire community, its transformative power can be truly amazing. Not only do
people become prayerful and worshipful and build
communities of believers, but many other changes
occur. People begin to live a different set of values
and practise a more just lifestyle. And hospitality,
sharing and participating become the new realities.

MEDITATION: *Where has the gospel done its transformative work in your life, family and wider community? Where is it still to penetrate?*

The power of love

'We have been created to love and to be loved.'
Mother Teresa

The blessing of being loved, cared for and affirmed can contribute to our being loving to others, generous and welcoming. But this is not always how it turns out. Sadly, the opposite can also occur. Those greatly loved can turn out to be selfish and demanding. This is simply one of the many ironies of life. There are those who come from emotionally deprived families who have turned out to be very caring for others. What this highlights is that it is not simply a matter of how much or how little we have received during our upbringing, but what we do with our lives through the ongoing choices we are making. In choosing to love we are also empowered to love.

REFLECTION: *Love is always risk-taking, for those to whom we seek to be loving are not always willing to receive, let alone to reciprocate.*

The whole person

'Mission is concerned with the development of the whole person and of all people. It includes, therefore, the shaping of a new lifestyle.'

C. René Padilla

We have long lived with the polarisation of various categories — body and soul, worship and work, church and world and ministry to those within the community of believers and those outside. We are now seeking to move beyond these polarisations in order to develop a much more holistic approach in ministry. The focus is on ministry to the whole person in the life settings where that person finds himself or herself. The concern is for the person's spiritual, social, intellectual and vocational development. And discipleship and formation is to shape people for their family, educational, vocational and spiritual tasks.

THOUGHT: *Holistic ministry has in view the shaping of a person for his or her role in any legitimate sphere of life so that all of life can be lived to the glory of God and the wellbeing of others.*

Dominion

'The purpose of God's saving activity is to restore man's dominion on earth.'

Vishal Mangalwadi

God's salvation is as comprehensive as it is generous. That it is generous is more than obvious. God extends his forgiveness and grace when we in no way deserve it and he welcomes us even though we have been disobedient and wayward. That God's salvation is comprehensive is not always fully understood or appreciated. Salvation includes not only spiritual blessing, but also protection, being rescued from difficulties and physical and material blessing. But there is so much more. God's salvation is not simply for individuals but for families, communities and even for the whole created order. Those who experience God's salvation are not called away from the world, but to work in it as vice-regents under God's rulership.

THOUGHT: *If we can work with God and under God's rulership, we may be able to make the world a more just place.*

Solidarity

'The more radical, difficult, or arduous a decision, the more need there is to feel the presence of other groups involved in the same risk.'

J.B.Libanio

When one is embedded in the smooth flow of continuity and tradition, one does not need to seek companions in the journey. They are already there. But this is not the case for those who swim against the tide; those who work for change; those who resist the old and dream and work for the new. They inevitably walk the lonely road. They are often misunderstood and frequently maligned. Theirs is the task not only to work for the new, but to build coalitions; to develop partnership; to create solidarity; to network; to join with others in the journey towards the new. Since a counter-consciousness can only be sustained in a counter-community, all those who work for change must be community builders.

PRAYER: *Lord, give me the grace to work with others in the furtherance of your kingdom.* Amen.

October

God will always respond much more favourably to our needs and struggles than to our strengths and competencies.

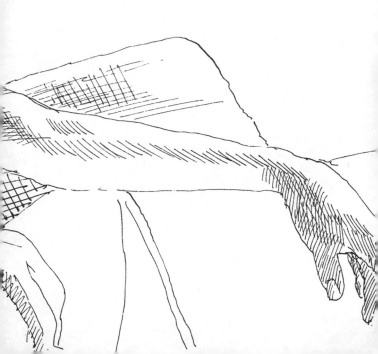

God will always respond much more generously
to our needs and struggles than to our strength
and self-reliance.

Proclamation and contemplation

'There is a Word which emerges out of silence.'

Rubem Alves

If only we would pray before we act. If only we would listen before we speak. If only we would worship before we serve. If only we would receive before we give. If only we would be still before we proclaim. If only we would identify before we give advice. If only we would become empty before we share our blessings. If only. . . The litany goes on and on. . . But what a difference these things could make in our lives and service. We need to learn to drink from our own wells before we attempt to carry water to others. We need to be still in order to hear. We need to have heard in order to speak. And our speaking must also come from our experience in practical service.

THOUGHT: *Those who have met with God can best speak on God's behalf.*

Prayer

'Prayer is not a pious instrument by which we move God to baptise our enterprises; it is entering the strength of him who moves history and binds the powers that be.'

Melba Maggay

Prayer is coming home. It is the place of rest, renewal and encouragement. It is the place of openness, honesty and vulnerability. It is the place where we can be the most true to ourselves and the most open about our weaknesses and needs. God will always respond much more favourably to our needs and struggles than to our strengths and competencies. Therefore, our relationship with God can be a nurturing and empowering one. God is both father and mother. God is both protector and sustainer. God acts on our behalf, but also empowers us to be responsible for our own lives and for those placed within the circle of our care.

PRAYER: *Lord, help me always to run to you for your grace, wisdom, direction and empowerment.* Amen.

Colossians 2: 2–3 October 3

Growth into maturity

'God. . . has put us in a particular family because he
wants us to experience. . . the particular disciplines
and instruction, difficulties and delights, pains and
pleasures we need in order to grow into maturity.'
Isabelo Magalit

We speak of God's providential care. Some believe
this to mean that God actually orders all the circumstances and situations of our lives. This, however, can easily conjure up the picture that we are
mere puppets on a string. This idea can undermine
personal responsibility. There is little doubt, however, that God can use all the circumstances of our
lives to mould and to challenge us. The particular
family we grew up in, the schools we attended, the
neighbourhoods in which we lived, the jobs we
had, the friends we made — all of these and much
more have impacted on our lives for both good and
ill. God's grace working in our lives helps us to
celebrate the good and to come to terms with what
is less than desirable.

REFLECTION: *It is not so much a matter of what has
happened to us, but what we have done with these
things.*

God and neighbour

'Christianity. . . is, first of all, the knowledge of God and, second, the service of God.'

Carmen Guerrero Nakpil

Our lives find their meaning and purpose in a complex set of relationships. These relationships span both the vertical and the horizontal dimensions of our lives. We stand in relationship to God and to people. We are called to worship God and to serve people. We are never called to worship people, but we are called to serve God. And one way to serve God is to show God's kindness to others. To care, encourage, nurture and build up others is one very practical way of expressing our commitment to God. Thus, we love others because we are loved. We forgive because we have been forgiven. We bless because we have been blessed.

THOUGHT: *To serve others is not only the way to bless them, but to bless ourselves as well. But above all, service makes glad the heart of God.*

Building the new

'This word of God. . . is a living word that brings with it awareness and demands. It makes [us] aware of what sin and grace are and of what must be resisted and what must be built up.'

Oscar Romero

God's word as law, prophetic challenge, poetic utterance, gospel or didactic statement has entered our world as a shaft of light. As such, it has exposed the nature of evil, the folly of so much of what we do, the reality of evil forces arraigned against us and the power of structural evil. But it has also shown us the beauty and power of nature, the good things in the human community, the power of forgiveness, the joy of celebration, the blessing of community, the virtue of the work for justice and the hope of God's kingdom. Empowered by this vision, we can attempt with God's help to build the new where the old has brought decay.

THOUGHT: *The new cannot be simply a reaction to the old, but a vision of new possibilities.*

Openness to God

'We must be marked by a heightened God con-
sciousness. Then all kinds of things will happen.'
Desmond Tutu

There must be no suggestion that only Christians are creative and innovative. Men and
women of no faith or other faiths can display
these characteristics. And when they do, they are
reflecting God's common grace at work in
human activity. But when people seek the God of
all wisdom and grace and rely on the power of
the Spirit, all sorts of amazing things can happen.
Then reconciliation occurs. Forgiveness is extended
to others. Enemies come to peaceful solutions.
Resources are shared. Divisions are broken
down. Community is built. Joy is experienced.
Hurts are healed. And thus the signs of God's
kingdom appear. When this happens, the God of
surprises has come amongst us.

MEDITATION: *Where are the signs of God's presence
in your life, family and community?*

The power of love

'If there's love, Christ is among them; he is love among them. And then they can do everything because love is what's going to change the world.'

Felipe, a campesino

What is it that is really going to make the significant difference in our world? Is it the use of strong political power? Is it the promotion of economic development? Is it the creation of equal opportunities for all? Is it the work of justice and the practice of love? Or is it all of the above and so much more? The answer is, that it takes a lot to change ourselves and our communities, let alone our world. Change is never simplistic or easy, but working for change involves the practice of love, since it provides the motive and direction of all of our strategies. We work with people for change because we want to bless them and do them good.

REFLECTION: *Actions that spring from love are always better motivated than actions that spring from reaction.*

The work of justice

'To establish justice is to remove everything that
hinders healthy relationships between people.'
Hugo Zorrila

We are aware that the work of justice has to do
with creating good laws and caring and responsive
institutions. But the work of justice should also
finally nestle in our interpersonal relationships,
families and neighbourhood communities. If
justice can be experienced at both the macro-
level and the micro-level, then the impact has
been holistic. Justice, among other things, has to
do with the breaking down of barriers that
separate people into classes and groups and which
prevent them from having access to equal opportunity. This involves the husband-wife relationship
or that of the pastor-layperson, as much as the
relationship between dominant culture groups
and ethnic minorities.

THOUGHT: *To provide equal opportunities for others
may mean relinquishing our time or resources or
options.*

Emptiness

'God cannot fill us if we are filled with ourselves.'
Thomas H. Green

Some people wrongly understand emptiness as self-negation. Others fear the notion of emptiness because in the removal of outward constraints and preoccupations their world may collapse. Others are reluctant to face themselves because they don't want to confront the poverty of their inner lives. But acknowledging our need is the only starting point to growth. And coming to a place of emptiness is essential to God's further action in our lives. There are many ways in which we can come to this place: repentance; relinquishment; openness; stillness. When God wants us to come with our questions and our pain, our achievements become redundant. Therefore, we need to walk the road of humility in our relationship with God so we can be filled with good things.

MEDITATION: *What do I need to let go because this is blocking God's further blessing in my life?*

Knowing

'Knowing is something beautiful. To the extent that knowing is unveiling an object, the unveiling gives the object life, calls it into life, even gives it new life.'

Paulo Freire

To know is much more than to have information about something. To know is to enter. But to enter involves being welcomed. We can never know another person unless he or she practises the gentle art of self-disclosure. And that openness and transparency is hardly likely to occur unless we are able to create a non-threatening environment and begin to build bridges of trust and vulnerability. But knowing is more than appreciating another's self-disclosure. Knowing also grasps what has not yet been revealed. In this way, knowing is unveiling. It intuitively explores what may be there, what could be said and what may possibly be disclosed. Knowledge involves naming and articulating what the other can then recognise and claim as his or her own.

REFLECTION: *To know involves more than inwardness and self-reflection. It also involves outwardness — the process of allowing ourselves to be known by others.*

Transformation

'While we are shaped by culture, we can also reshape and transform culture.'

Josue Ganibe

Every society needs its secular dissidents and its religious prophets. Sometimes these two groups of people annunciate a common theme, even though their use of language may be quite different. That this occurs is due to the fact that religious prophets are also part of the human community. They hear and speak the concerns of God, not only for the community of believers, but also for the general society. On the other hand, secular prophets and activists are often not without spiritual insight. Where church and society meet in seeking to bring about social change, the force for renewal may be unstoppable. Sadly, sometimes the secular prophets have relevant things to say, but the church is not listening. Sometimes, and equally sadly, the religious prophets are voices crying in the wilderness. But if we hear and act to both one or the other, we may be the leaven for change that society urgently needs.

THOUGHT: *To break loose from dominant cultural values requires a powerful alternative vision.*

Nurture

'There is no great man in the world who did not pass through the nurturing hands of a woman.'

Grace Eneme

Jesus was born of a woman. Mary nurtured and cared for him. She succored him. She may well have been his confidante and friend. That she continued to care deeply for her special son is beyond doubt. That she was grieved by his rejection and death is obvious. And that he was her saviour is the declaration of faith. That Mary played an important role in the life of Jesus goes well beyond carrying him in pregnancy. She may well have shaped his life and formed his constructive relationships with women. That Jesus had a liberating attitude to women is writ large in the Gospels. And it is this attitude of inclusivity that has provided inspiration for women and men to work beyond cultural and role stereotypes, leading to true partnership.

THOUGHT: *If women and men can work in partnership, making their respective contributions, then we can build a gentler world.*

Conflict and growth

'There is no Christian — or human — maturity and there is no development of an adult spirituality without passage through the crises of conflict.'

Segundo Galilea

It is obvious that we benefit from all the good things that have come our way through family, friends, education, work, the community of believers and through opportunities to serve others. Good things can make us good, not simply satiated or selfish. And it is obvious that we don't always benefit from the bad things that come our way. Through them we can become paralysed or embittered. But the bad can also be a blessing in disguise. Difficulty can make us stronger. It can also make us more sensitive to the needs of others. And difficulty can deepen our relationship with God because we are no longer worshipping the God who only blesses us, but also the God who sustains us through the darkness.

MEDITATION: *Come in touch with how a crisis has enriched your life.*

Spirit and empowerment

'When the poor succeed in becoming agents in history, then the Spirit of God is at work.'

José Comblin

The Spirit of God is the creative Spirit and the empowering Spirit. The Spirit always bursts out of the programs, structures and institutions that we create and so jealously maintain. This is not to suggest that the Spirit is anti-institutional, but that the Spirit renews all that we do and create. The Spirit is also the just Spirit and the Spirit of the poor. The Spirit never empowers the powerful when their position is used to exploit and marginalise others. Rather, the Spirit lifts up the lowly and gives them dignity, hope and a future. One of the signs that the Spirit is at work is when sinners are forgiven, the bitter extend forgiveness, the alienated are reconciled, the hurt are healed, the needy receive help, the poor are empowered, community is created and justice reigns.

PRAYER: *Lord, may your renewing Spirit do these things in our lives and communities.* Amen.

Encounter

'Every spirituality receives its initial impulse from an encounter with the Lord.'

Gustavo Gutiérrez

The genius of Christian spirituality is not primarily a set of dogmas or a certain kind of religious institution. Nor is it primarily the worship of a distant and remote Being. Instead, Christian spirituality has to do with encounter and presence which in turn leads to transformation and service. At the heart of this spirituality is the amazing move of God towards us in Jesus Christ which results in embrace, forgiveness and celebration. This initial embrace issues in the joy of presence. God journeys with us in the midst of life. And it is this journeying together that leads to our gradual transformation. We are changed by the gentle hand of God. Out of this ongoing transformation comes the joy of service where we seek to bless others in the way we have been blessed.

REFLECTION: *Christ in us. . . Christ ahead of us. . . we can journey with the Christ who has embraced us and leads the way into our world.*

Withdrawal

'I do understand about withdrawing to pray in the wilds, provided you take all the cares, preoccupations and problems afflicting humanity with you.'

Dom Helder Camara

A fine and difficult balance exists between meeting our own emotional and spiritual needs and the needs of others. To meet our own needs we need to be nurtured and encouraged. But we also need to find quietude, silence and peace. Out of stillness can come new energies and hope. But we need to come down from the mountain of blessing and mingle with the hurting of our world, enter into their pain and bring God's healing and peace. In turning away from the world, we turn to God in order to be nurtured and empowered. And in facing the world, we seek to bring the blessings we encountered in our solitude.

REFLECTION: *Solitude is not marking time; it is renewing inner resources.*

Relevance

'What is the value of a Christianity in which Jesus is worshipped as Lord, but Christian discipleship— "the way of Jesus" — is regarded as largely ir- relevant to life in the modern world?'

C. René Padilla

The lordship of Christ is a confession of faith. It is also an affirmation of great possibilities since we live in the hope that Christ's lordship will become more evident in our lives, churches and society. It is, therefore, not only a matter of a declaration of faith, but also lived experience expressed in a life of obedience and service. And if we are seeking to live out the implications of Christ's lordship in our per- sonal lives, we also have to explore what this means for our families, neighbourhoods, the church, the workplace and society. Since Christ can be lord of a business as well as a family, we are left with the challenging task to explore what that will look like in the practical realities of life.

THOUGHT: *Christianity is not a world-denying but a world-formative religion.*

Songs in the night

'It is one of the mysteries of the human heart that those who have the most always want more. . . while those who have the least come to terms with their lot. . . [and] sing.'

Emmanuelle Cinquin

Sociologists have characterised the West as a culture of complaint, even though it is a culture of material prosperity. By contrast, the Third World is typified as a culture of hope, even though a significant proportion of its people live in abject and degrading poverty. Those in the slums of Metro Manila get on with their lives with quiet determination. And when fire destroys their community, they are rebuilding the same day. And despite the fact that they have so little, they are generous and know the abandoning art of celebration. In the midst of death, they know how to dance. Inspite of the overwhelming odds against them, they have not given way to despair, but live to embrace a better day.

REFLECTION: *Much having makes life more convenient, it does not necessarily make it richer.*

Start at home

'Start at home, start among your own people. They are in need. . . harassed. . . dejected. . . oppressed. . . Start with them, casting out and curing.'

Joseph G. Donders

We don't have to travel far to find people in need. They may be within our family. They may be neighbours or work colleagues. And we don't have to look too hard to find the poor, ethnic minorities, people with a disability, or others who have been marginalised in our society. Overcoming our own selfishness will always be an issue in ministering to such people. Overcoming our fears is another and so is finding appropriate ways to join and journey with those who are in difficulty. And overcoming our lack of inner resources is a pressing issue. People don't always need material help. They also need encouragement, healing, deliverance and empowerment. And this is where the question comes close to home: do we have the spiritual power to impart the blessings that people seek and need?

THOUGHT: *To be what we need to be for people, we first need to be with God.*

Compassion and care

'The warmth of love and friendship, the capacity to
understand what others need, are as necessary for
life as medicine and monthly welfare cheques.'
Arturo Paoli

While the Third World still has its primary
structures of care through family and neighbourhood, the First World has created secondary
structures through the provision of many professional services. While the latter may provide ex-
cellent help, we need more than professional care
to become whole. Friendship. Informal help and
care. The experience of community. Practical assistance. Good advice. Intercessory prayers. Welcome. Understanding and acceptance. Presence.
These things, among others, can enrich our lives
and sustain us in the long journey. Therefore,
while we may not be able to give much in the
form of professional help, the human gift of
solidarity can be truly empowering.

THOUGHT: *Give of who you are, not only of what
you have.*

Struggle

'We learned that getting what we are struggling for may not be the most important thing. We may not get what we're after. But getting it isn't as important as the act of struggling for it.'

Niall O'Brien

Of course, we all want our hopes and dreams to come to fulfilment. And we want the projects for which we have laboured so hard to be successful. We want our efforts to change things in society to have good outcomes. And we long to see a better and more just world. That all of these good things don't fully happen is hardly a reason for despair, indifference or resignation. The work of transformation is seldom the work of success. It is the work of struggle. But much more importantly, it is the work of faithfulness. We must do what we must because the sheer injustice of the situation cries out for a response. And in making that response, we pray and plan, work and network, act and react and become more proactive and entrust all to the grace and mercy of God. And when nothing much has changed, we try again.

REFLECTION: *The work of justice is the impulse to new life.*

Fear

'Having fear is a manifestation of being alive. I don't have to hide my fears. But, what I cannot permit is that my fear is unjustified, immobilising me.'
Paulo Freire

The brightest, the most capable and the most dedicated among us can become sidetracked and disempowered. Burnout and disillusionment are frequent factors. While the former may be caused by overwork and the inability to set boundaries and limits, the latter may be caused by goal displacement or being the victims of institutional 'violence' where the organisation has failed to nurture us. But there are also other factors that can immobilise us. The interminable struggle to see a more just society. The irresolution of our own difficulties. The re-emergence of old fears and the mocking presence of new ones. The list could go on. What all of this highlights is our own need for care and nurture. Our need to face the things that come against us. Our need to be courageous. But above all, our need to be watchful and prayerful.

REFLECTION: *Our fears often have to do with what other people think. While we should never ignore others, we do need to be faithful to our own convictions.*

1 Corinthians 5: 9–13   **October 23**

Being salt

'It seems to m   that the salt has got lost when, instead of preserving justice on earth, Christians have let injustice multiply more.'

Olivia, a campesina

Most Christians, unless they have been influenced by a world-denying gospel, do strive to work for good in the world. They happily acknowledge that the love and grace of God motivates them to bless others. The big question, however, is how can one best do good in our world. Rather than advocating single strategies, a multiple approach is called for. Making an impact on society does involve building strong families. It also involves building dynamic communities of faith among every strata of society. But Christians are also called to build institutions that serve society such as hospitals, schools and social welfare services, as well as to redeem existing services that have suffered neglect. And of course Christians are called to make their presence felt in the arts as much as in politics.

THOUGHT: *The challenge is to let our light shine in the places where we find ourselves. It also means going to places where the need is great.*

Matthew 26: 69–75   **October 24**

The enemy within

'Our main problem lies within ourselves, and with our difficulty to be faithful and to be obedient, to love justice and mercy and to walk humbly with our Lord.'

Allan Boesak

That there are powers arraigned against us, is stating the obvious. And if one has never experienced this, then it is highly likely that such a person has not sought to live for the kingdom of God. For in seeking to do God's good in our world, we are threatened by evil spirits and by the evil that exists in the institutions we are seeking to change. But sadly, the picture is much more complicated. Evil also lies within us, including those who seek to do good and to be change agents. As a result, we can be arrogant, one-sided and wrong in our analysis of wrongs that need to be righted. Moreover, we can be self-righteous and impatient or fearful and ineffective. Thus in seeking to change the world, we would do well to first change ourselves and do the work of justice with humility.

MEDITATION: *Do you dare to identify the evil within as readily as the enemy without?*

Revelation 7: 9–10   **October 25**

Cooperation

'All the sounds must be mobilised in the great symphony of the Hallelujah Chorus, to be heard not only in heaven, but on earth.'

Shoki Coe

Christians live in the hope of the resurrection and the coming of the new heaven and earth. There sickness and death will not be found and all the saints will join in the triumphant chorus to our God and to our saviour and lord, Jesus Christ. This hope in a totally new reality can inspire us to work towards its coming. This does not mean that we can bring God's final kingdom here through our efforts and ministry. Only God can establish that kingdom. But we can work and pray to make it as much as a reality as possible. We can work for reconciliation and peace and establish communities of sharing and care and work for justice in our divided world. These then are the signposts of the greater reality that awaits our beautiful yet broken world. There God will be all in all and we will come to a true place of worship.

THOUGHT: *Celebration here is the foretaste of the great celebration to come.*

The laity

'Lay people are discovering their importance; they, too, are successors of the apostles in that they have inherited the apostolic teachings and are co-responsible for the unity of faith and the community.'

Leonardo Boff

While there are sections in scripture that stress the importance of pastoral leaders, the New Testament also knows a radical egalitarianism. All those incorporated by faith in Jesus Christ, whether they be men or women, the well to do or those on the bottom of the social ladder, the capable and the strugglers, have a part to play in the community of faith. Since all have natural gifts, life experiences and skills and all have spiritual gifts, all can contribute to the well-being of the community. And since we can't see the bigger picture without the help of the other, we need the wisdom and input of others. And since we all have weaknesses as well as strengths we need to receive ministry from others even while we seek to serve the community.

MEDITATION: *How can I best serve others? Where do I need the help of others?*

Clarity

'The clarity of the mystic and the prophet is not
very common. Most of us live in the to and fro of an
oscillation, a swinging of the pendulum between
clarity and confusion.'

J. B. Libanio

We do have flashes of insight. Inspiration. Wisdom.
And clarity regarding some problem or a future
direction. But inspiration is not our daily bread.
In the rough and tumble of life, torn between many
options and subject to many pressures, clarity often
aludes us and decision-making is difficult. As a
result, we sometimes take a leap without having
thought things through or we hesitate and remain
moribund and immobilised. But we do need to
make choices and decisions and for this clarity is an
important ingredient. If this doesn't come through
intuitive insight, it will need to come through struggle, discussion, questioning, advice-seeking and
agonising prayer.

THOUGHT: *To know where one is going and what
one should do is a great gift of insight.*

Confrontation

'Those who seek to confront the powers that be are likely to experience the full force of the enemy.'

Melba Maggay

Anyone who has sought to do the work of justice and has confronted evil and has sought to work for change, talks in hushed tones about the awesome strength of the powers of this age. Those who blithely claim victory are hardly realistic. Because the powers of this age are embedded in social structures and institutions controlled by the elite in a society, the work of justice will always evoke opposition. For justice calls for the human dignity of all. Equal opportunity. Fraternity. Solidarity. Community. Justice calls for an evangelical poverty of the rich — that is, downward mobility through the sharing of resources for the sake of the gospel. It calls for the upliftment of the poor through strategies that empower, give responsibility and provide choices. Any attempt that promotes this dual movement of downward mobility and upliftment will receive opposition, including from those within the community of faith.

THOUGHT: *Social activists are quickly branded as communists and equally quickly experience rejection by the social elite and major sections of the Christian church.*

Luke 19: 1-9   **October 29**

Salvation

'Salvation is not a purely immaterial question, it is a concrete reality in the here and now of real life.'
Juan Sepulveda

God doesn't only save our soul. The whole person is renewed by the grace of God. While inner spiritual renewal is foundational, the action of God within us radiates to every aspect of who we are. The grace and wisdom of God renew the mind. The healing power of God can renew our innermost being as well as our body. God's transformative work affects our relationships and builds community in places where previously there was discord and division. The concrete reality of physical healing, the creation of communities of faith and sharing and the hope of the resurrection of the body and the creation of new heavens and a renewed earth, all demonstrate God's concern for the total person and for all of reality.

THOUGHT: *If no part of our life is outside the grace of God, then all of life can be marked by the goodness of God.*

Romans 15: 1-6   **October 30**

Community

'The community meetings bound us closer and closer together. The doors were open. We said hello to one another, we went to one another's houses. For the first time, this scattered people was united.'
Pablo Galdámez

We all experience being scattered. In the First World, people are alienated from their families and their neighbourhoods. In the Third World people are deeply rooted in their families, but are initially suspicious of outsiders. The challenge facing all of us is to be gathered. In being gathered to the God of grace who welcomes us in our need and embraces us in love, new possibilities emerge. If we are forgiven, we can forgive others. If we are blessed, we can extend blessing. If we are welcomed, we can extend hospitality to others. And so there opens up the possibility of building community that overcomes our previous divisions. The road to community is not so much bound up with new structures, but new relationships of openness and sharing.

THOUGHT: *Community is always the work of the Spirit who brings people together in Jesus Christ.*

Interdependence

'We are made for a delicate network of relationships of interdependence. We are meant to complement each other.'

Desmond Tutu

Interdependence is a journey. It is not a gift. It is something we work towards. And as such, it is first of all the move beyond a prideful sense of independence where we come to recognise that we ourselves do not possess everything that is necessary for the task. This means that we recognise what we can contribute and what we lack. It involves acknowledging our giftedness and our limitations. Secondly, the journey to interdependence involves the gentle art of connecting. It involves joining with others and inviting them to contribute to the entire process. This means that they become part of the planning process as well the implementation. Thus the journey to interdependence involves giving up control so that others can make their meaningful contribution.

THOUGHT: *To do things alone is to violate the rhythm of life which has its genesis in connecting and is sustained through mutual nourishment.*

November

*The gospel is good news
for the weary, the broken
and the disempowered.*

The shaping of a life

'We must. . . let ourselves be evangelised, accept the good news of the merciful goodness of God and let ourselves be shaped by it to the point of making our own mercy its manifestation and channel.'

Juan Ramón Moreno

The gospel is good news for the weary, the broken and the disempowered. This is because the gospel, when embraced, does not leave us where we are. It transforms us. It brings us close to God's heart. It cleanses our sin. It lances our hurt. It fills us with hope. But the gospel not only transforms us, but reshapes our life. With the good news ringing in our ears and the good Spirit residing in our heart, we can live a different set of values. We can begin to treat others in the same generous way in which God has treated us.

THOUGHT: *The power of the gospel lies not only in its ability to change us, but also in its impact on others whose lives we are privileged to influence.*

Receiving and giving

'These are humble women who are open to community from their own experience of solitude, and who enrich it with the gifts they have been given freely and who learn to give freely what they have received.'

Consuelo Del Prado

Whoever we are, male or female, young or old, mainstream or marginalised, we cannot live life against itself. What I mean by this is that life has certain rhythms and realities that cannot be violated lest we do violence to ourselves. Sleep is as necessary as work. Rest is as important as activity. Affirmation is needed just as much as challenge. Prayer is as important as planning. The practice of solitude is as necessary as participating in community. And the gracious art of receiving is as important as the gift of generosity and giving.

REFLECTION: *The joy of wellbeing is premised on the blessing of harmony. And harmony has to do with living life consistently within its own inner designs.*

Self-understanding

'I have learned from the poor how poor I myself am.'
Mother Teresa

In God's light, we see light. In God's embrace, we know ourselves to be loved and forgiven. In the acceptance that a friend gives us, we know ourselves to be worthwhile. In the gentle care of the other, we know ourselves to be precious. Thus, in the face of the other person, we discover things about ourselves. In the positive action of others towards us we are affirmed and encouraged. But we also learn from those who are different from us. From the opposite sex, from someone with different social status and from someone with different values we can discover new things and also things about ourselves that we have failed to recognise before. Therefore, the other is always God's gentle gift to us.

THOUGHT: *Particularly from those who are very different, we can discover the hidden parts of ourselves.*

The liberating word

'The Word of God. . . alone has the force sufficient
to conquer the forces of evil which corrupt life.'
Carlos Mesters

There are many ways by which we can make the
Word of God ineffective. We can make it subservient to our own traditions. We can doubt or
rationalise its precepts and promises. We can
question the Word of God, but not be willing to
learn from it. But the Word of God can work its
own magic. While we are most obviously blessed
when we listen to it in faith and obedience, God's
Word is never mute or powerless. It has transformative power. Its gentle whispers or its disturbing
confrontation can revolutionise our inner world.
Like a shaft of light, it can lay bare our innermost
secrets. But it can also bring healing and encouragement and provide for us a vision of life that will
keep us focussed and purposeful.

REFLECTION: *The Word of God possesses a wisdom
that will guide us in the ways of truth and life.*

Starting again

'A critical skill we need to teach ourselves and our people is how to fail — how to learn our lessons from the experience of defeat and pick ourselves up again and start anew.'

Melba Maggay

There is nothing particularly virtuous about failure. But it is a reality of life, no matter how hard we work in order to succeed. Failure can occur for many reasons: lack of foresight; lack of planning; lack of resources; lack of courage. This list may be endless, but each failure may well have its own peculiar reasons, or even its lack of reasons. But failure need never be the end. It may simply be an acknowledgement of our vulnerability and fragility and that the realities of life are so much bigger and more complex than we had ever imagined. Failure, therefore, is always an invitation to start again — but not in the same way. Failure beckons us to attempt the new out of the ashes of the old.

PRAYER: *Lord, may failure not immobilise me, but may it spur me to learn its lessons and to try again.* Amen.

Prayer and action

'Don't ask God to solve the problem. . . of discord among human beings, but use prayer to break out of your own shell — to come out of yourself and move toward someone else.'

Arturo Paoli

There are things which God alone can do. There are also things that we must do. We cannot leave our responsibilities to God just as God does not expect us to do what is humanly impossible. This is particularly the case in the difficult work of reconciliation. When we have offended others, we need to make peace. When others have offended us, we need to seek peace just as much. We cannot hope for problems resulting from relationship breakdown simply to go away. They may well get worse, resulting in avoidance or bitterness. We therefore need to take action and become peacemakers even as we pray for God to prepare the way and to give us hearts of humility and openness.

MEDITATION: *Prayerfully reflect on which person you may need to approach in order to undo past damage.*

Compromise

'In matters of peace-building, there are only few instances where there is no room for flexibility and the humility of compromise if all factors are taken into account.'

Niall O'Brien

In the challenging work of bringing about community change, no single interest group has all the answers. Since we all have our vested interests and our own agendas, we see the needs and the struggles of the community in a particular light. And because we operate within a particular ideological framework, we also have our possible answers and solutions. Since the issues are always bigger than any one of us, we need to commit ourselves to hearing from others and seek, in the to and fro movement of dialogue, to come to a bigger and better understanding of the challenges and opportunities which confront us. This dialectic of question and answer always means that new things are added to our existing insights, while some things which we are no longer defensible are relinquished.

Matthew 5: 9   **November 8**

The triumph of freedom

'Oppression and injustice and suffering can't be the end of the human story. Freedom and justice, peace and reconciliation are God's will for all of us, black and white.'

Desmund Tutu

We know that, finally, evil cannot triumph. There is the promise of a new age where righteousness and peace will reign supreme. That this may soon come should be in our hearts and in our prayers. The triumph of evil in our present world is intolerable. We cannot be passive in the face of evil. Evil is ugly. It scars the image of God in our lives. It dehumanises us. And it perverts God's will and purpose for humankind. Therefore, we are called to cooperate with God's passion for justice and peace. Being changed by the grace of God, we give ourselves to the task of being peacemakers in our world, no matter what that may personally cost us.

THOUGHT: *If justice and peace are God's will, then we may be confident that God will sustain us in the work of justice.*

---

1 Peter 3: 9–12   **November 9**

Calling

'Men and women are called by God to a specific task, a *vocation*, which they are expected to fulfil with wholehearted obedience and faithfulness.'

Adonis Gorospe

The idea of calling is often applied only to those who are called to a particular office or ministry in the community of believers. But this emasculates the concept. We are *all* called to faith in Christ and this calling opens to us a new world of possibilities. Christ transforms us and empowers with gifts and abilities and calls us to serve him in faithfulness and obedience wherever we may find ourselves. As a consequence, one is called to be a servant of Christ as a medical doctor or a teacher just as much as a pastor or a priest. But the issue is much deeper. It is not simply a matter of being called to a particular task or job. It is being called to be a certain kind of person with certain values that glorify Christ and empower others that constitutes the heart of God's call.

THOUGHT: *To have a sense of calling gives our life a sense of direction.*

The silence of God

'God remains silent so that men and women may speak, protest and struggle.'

Elsa Tamez

God has spoken clearly in covenant and promise, in priest and prophet, in law and gospel. Most clearly, God has spoken in his son, Jesus Christ. In all these ways, God has spoken paradigmatically and we are called to repeat and apply all that God has spoken in the past. Therefore, we don't need a new word when relationships break down and when barriers of bitterness are erected. We don't need a new word about being peacemakers; community builders; healers; workers for justice; empowering the poor. God has clearly called us to be this and so much more in our world. Therefore, we must speak and we must act and, above all, we must pray that our speaking and acting will have its desired effects.

REFLECTION: *God has empowered us to be his spokespersons and servants in our broken world.*

The greater good

'To simply renounce evil is not Christian spirituality;
Christian spirituality goes beyond this. It leads us
occasionally to renounce even the legitimate in
order better to imitate Jesus.'

Segundo Galilea

The genius of the Christian life is not cast in
negative terms. It is not simply a matter of what we
should not do or avoid. It is, instead, an affirmation
of life; a passion to follow Jesus; a desire to please
God in all we do; a vision to build a better world; a
concern to care for our fragile environment; a commitment to do good and to champion the cause of justice.
In living out this positive vision, we will need more
than enthusiasm. We will need to be women and
men of faith; hope; prayer; courage; endurance. But
we will also need to be men and women who are
prepared to deny ourselves, to relinquish what
may be legitimately ours and to walk the second
mile.

MEDITATION: *Identify what you may need to let go
for the sake of the kingdom of God.*

Blessing

'Blessing. . . has as its basic principle God's gracious or favourable will toward us. Blessing is a gift that touches life and its mystery.'

Judette A. Gallares

A blessing is performative language. It is not a mere wish or a vague hope. It is a declaration of what is and what will be. God's blessing is not a magic word of comfort in the midst of hopelessness. Instead, it is the active presence of God in our circumstances. And when God comes amongst us, God's hands are never empty. They are full of the blessings and gifts we need to face life and to live it to the full. This does not mean that God's blessings are always material resources. Sometimes, we simply receive the gift of presence. At other times, it may be gift of faith or perseverance; or peace; or hope. But there are also the blessings of God's deliverance and help and provision.

REFLECTION: *Blessing is hardly something that comes to us by way of demand. It is the surprise that makes life full.*

Intuition and critical thinking

'I think that imagination, guessing, intuition, cannot be dichotomised from critical thinking.'

Paulo Freire

If we are to be involved in the urgent task of social transformation, then we need to understand the kind of world in which we live. This understanding must not only be impressionistic, but also analytical and critical. We need to look at the social shape of our local communities as well as the mega-factors that shape social reality. But the task of coming to understanding involves more than critical analysis. It involves exposure, sympathy, journeying with, joining and care. More importantly, it involves dreaming and visioning as we look for solutions, answers and new possibilities. The task of social transformation has finally to do with the creative imagination that anticipates the new, coupled with careful planning and the courage to do the hard work.

THOUGHT: *Seeing creative possibilities has to do with careful analysis, but also with group brainstorming and prayer.*

Sharing

'It's easy to share your meal with a friend. It's harder to share with people you don't know.'

Alejandro, a campesina

Naturally, we are to open our hearts and our hands to our friends. That is what friendship is all about. It is being with, journeying together, openness, trust and practical sharing. These kinds of friendships are important for they affirm us, nurture us and empower us for our role in the world. It is because we have a circle of friends that we can welcome the stranger. It is because we receive good things from our friends that we are able to give to others. In that sense, it is not difficult to give to those whom we don't know. We are able to connect up with others when we ourselves are embedded in relationships and in a community of love and care.

THOUGHT: *It is one thing to be a caring and giving person. It is another to create caring communities which welcome the broken and alienated of our world.*

Relevance

'One of the most important ways in which committed Christians can help people is by encouraging them to take their religious values and beliefs out of mothballs and integrate them into the part of their lives where they are actively living.'

Donal Dorr

God's good news has relevance for every aspect of our lives. Not only is there direction and guidance on how we are to live our life with God, but there is also wisdom for living the life of faith in our challenging world. There is wisdom for family and church life, daily work, being neighbours and relating to the state. There are insights on relationship, the process of reconciliation, power and leadership issues, the task of peacemaking and the work of justice. When these good things are embedded in our own lives and in communities of believers and are translated into the affairs of daily life, then we may well make a significant impact on our world.

THOUGHT: *A faith lived is a vital faith.*

The freedom of the Spirit

'We cannot try to harness the energy of the Spirit for a particular end, no matter how good or how urgent it may seem.'

Thomas H. Green

Receiving the Spirit does not mean that we possess the Spirit. In fact, it is the other way round. The Spirit possesses us. But that possession is never a form of control. The Spirit guides, enlightens, empowers, endows and beautifies. The Spirit works with grace and sensitivity. The Spirit nudges and encourages us. The Spirit always looks for our response and cooperation. When it comes to our relationship to the Spirit, we cannot use the Spirit for our own ends. The Spirit is linked to the Word of God, is given to magnify Christ, is the creative activity of God and enhances and advances the concerns of God's kingdom. The Spirit cooperates with us when we are committed to these concerns.

REFLECTION: *When we are passionate about God's concerns, the Spirit will empower us. When we are not on about those concerns, we are probably working in our own strength.*

Priesthood of all believers

'Every Christian is invited to view his or her function, profession, abilities as gifts that have been received and that must be exercised in service to the entire community.'

Leonardo Boff

We are called by God to build the two communities — the community of believers and the human community. The call to build the one is not higher than the call to build the other. Thus, the task of parenting is not higher or lower than that of pastoral care or other forms of ministry in the community of believers. Whatever our giftedness and ability, our job or profession, we can finds ways to serve God wherever we may find ourselves in the marketplace, in the home, in church, or in other institutional settings. The farmer serves the human community just as much as the engineer and both may serve God as much as the pastor or priest in their vocations.

THOUGHT: *If we are willing to serve, we are all able to make a contribution to the two communities.*

Solidarity

'Solidarity with others is premised on a death somewhere within us.'

Melba Maggay

Just as saying goodbye is a little dying, so letting
go is a little dying as well. And solidarity is the
gentle art of letting go of some of our own
dreams, ideas and plans. This is not to suggest
that our letting go should be cheap and easy. If
we do this, we may well lose our integrity and
together with others sink to some beggarly
common denominator. Instead, letting go
should occur in the light of better dreams and
plans. Thus, solidarity is built in the to and fro
movement of dialogue where we both make our
contribution and also receive from others. In the
process of committing ourselves to the bigger
dream, we may well experience a sense of joy
and a sense of loss.

THOUGHT: *A little dying is a form of extending ourselves.*

The unloved

'Right in your midst there are those who suffer because they do not feel [they are] wanted or loved.'

Mother Teresa

We may think that we are doing well in loving and serving the members of our family. We believe that each one is important and therefore we give them special time and attention. We respect differences and, as a result, are aware of the fact that they have differing needs. But no matter how attentive and careful we may be, we may still fail. And we most easily fail with those who are the least demanding, the most giving and who most readily fit in with the demands of others. These we can take for granted. And because they have established this accommodating way of operating, they may not be able to articulate their real needs and, even when they do, we may not be able to hear.

REFLECTION: *We don't need to look very far in finding those whom we have failed to love to the extent of their need.*

Conversion

'Personal conversion, however, cannot be authentic without the action for freedom and justice and truth and love. To be really liberating, conversion must practically be conversion to God and our brothers and sisters.'

Fausto Gomez

Conversion involves a change of mind and of life direction. In turning to God, we embrace his wisdom and forgiveness. We acknowledge his rulership in our lives and seek to live to his glory. This central transformation should have all kinds of implications. To put that differently, it should lead to further conversions. Our minds, values and concerns need to be reorientated. We need to abandon our old ways of doing things and embrace the concerns of God's kingdom. This means that conversion becomes a way of life, not a once-for-all experience.

MEDITATION: *Conversion is not simply a matter of turning away from something. It is much more a matter of turning towards the new. What is the new that you need to embrace?*

The whole

'The great need today is for a restoration of a fuller perspective on God's activity in terms of his mission of the kingdom. We have become caught up in trying to put together all the pieces to make up the whole rather than in attempting to grasp the whole itself.'

Ken Gnanakan

The relationship between the part and the whole is what we call the hermeneutic circle. This circle works dynamically. Words, for example, make up a sentence. This is the movement from parts to the whole. But the words can only be understood in the light of the sentence, the whole. All of life is lived in this dynamic. Life is most meaningful and purposeful when we can grasp something of the bigger picture. This is equally true in living the Christian life. And the ultimate big picture is to know something of the purposes of God in history and beyond — in the coming and outworking of his reign of love, peace and justice in our world and in the world to come.

PRAYER: *Lord, open our minds and hearts so that we may move beyond our petty perspectives to see more of your kingdom. Amen.*

Psalm 85: 8–13   **November 22**

Faith

'Faith. . . is the conviction that something can and will happen because it is good and because it is true that goodness can and will triumph over evil.'

Albert Nolan

Some would hold that to have faith in the triumph of good over evil is to have a naive faith. It is a faith which negates the radicality of evil in our world. It is the faith of a sugar-coated liberalism with its humanistic optimism. But all of this need not be the case. To have faith in the triumph of good over evil does not mean that *we* will achieve this. That viewpoint is naive. Since we cannot banish evil from our own lives, we can hardly banish it from our world.

And since our communities of believers are hardly pure, we all continue to contribute to the pain of our world. Therefore, the triumph of good over evil is always the triumph of *God's* grace and action in our lives and world.

MEDITATION: *Can you identify an incident where God's grace was triumphant in the face of all odds and celebrate that with thankfulness and joy?*

John 16: 12–15   November 23

Truth

'To speak the truth is to transcend both self and national interests and to give allegiance to God.'

Naim Stifan Ateek

So often, our sense of the truth is linked to our own values and ideas. In that sense, truth becomes *my* truth. And this understanding of truth may be suspect because we are always driven by our own interests and concerns. But truth is much more than simply our own possession;

it is also something that is disclosed to us. Thus, truth comes to us by way of revelation. Truth is the surprise. Truth awakens us. It beckons us. It confronts us. It seeks to take us by the hand and leads us in a direction where we may not want to go, but need to. Therefore, truth is frequently the unwelcome friend who serves us the best if only we will listen.

THOUGHT: *To hear the truth, we often need to hear things which are against ourselves.*

The cross

'The cross is a symbol reminding the world that God is at God's strongest when God seems to be at God's weakest.'

Choan-Seng Song

In one sense, God is never weak. God is all-powerful. But God chooses to work with people and in the world in ways that seem to limit his power. God, for example, called Israel to be a light to the nations. To the extent that Israel failed to let its light shine, the purposes of God appear to have been frustrated. Similarly, God has chosen to work through the church (this is not to deny that God also works apart from the church) and to the extent that the church is faithful to the purposes of God, God's power is released. But if the church is lacking in obedience and commitment, then God's work is hindered. But we are touching a mystery. God still works magnificently, even though all appears to be lost.

THOUGHT: *God cannot be put in a box. And we don't have the last word. So look out!*

Riches

'I know how very hard it is to be rich and still keep the milk of human kindness. Money has a dangerous way of putting scales on one's eyes, a dangerous way of freezing people's hands, eyes, lips and heart.'

Dom Helder Camara

I have met both in the First World and the Third World. There are those who are rich and generous. There are also those who are rich and full of avarice. This suggests that the problem lies not so much with having much, but what this does to us and what we do with the material blessings we have received. Clearly for some, much having has blinded them to the realities of the kingdom of God and they have closed their hearts to the call of God and the cry of their neighbour. Others have allowed riches to blind them to the need for social justice and they have become oppressive and exploitative. But for others, much having has resulted in the joy of responsible stewardship and care for the needy.

REFLECTION: *We cannot simply live for ourselves if we want to live to the glory of God.*

Romans 5: 18   **November 26**

Radical evil

'Because sin is radical evil, it can be conquered only by the grace of God and the radical liberation that the Lord bestows.'

Gustavo Gutiérrez

While we should never adopt a dark, pessimistic perspective on life where everything is regarded as evil, we should not treat sin lightly, either. Its effects are evident in our personal lives, families, communities and world. Thank God that we have not been left to our own devices. God has unleashed powerful redemptive forces in our world. These go back to the world of the patriarchs and the prophets and to Jesus Christ and the coming of the Spirit in power. These forces are also present in our world. They bring reconciliation; freedom; liberation; empowerment.

The triumph of the grace of God not only stems the tide of evil, but creates the good in our broken world.

PRAYER: *Lord, thank you for your preserving and transforming power in our lives and our world. Amen.*

James 2: 14–17   **November 27**

Deeds

'God has expressed his love for the whole of mankind in deeds rather than in words.

Ramon Bautista

Love will always find a way to express itself in specific and concrete ways. Love knows nothing about a selfish withholding. It does know about engagement, connecting and giving. The reason why love is so expressive is because its motivation is to bless and empower the object of our love. This does not mean that we do anything and everything for the one we love. But it does mean that we will do anything that will do good to the other. This pattern of operating finds its inspiration in the way that God so generously expresses love and concern for us. The ultimate expression of that concern was the gift of God's Son who gave his life as a ransom for many.

REFLECTION: *In the generous gift and the costly deed we see something of the heart of the giver.*

Matthew 24: 45–51   November 28

Ultimate realities

'For faith there is no merely natural, neutral order outside the scope of grace and sin. Everything we do, even our smallest act, whether or not it consciously refers to God, is related to salvation or perdition.'

Leonardo Boff

Spirituality is not a sphere that is marked off from other areas of life. Spirituality, or the lack thereof, affects every aspect of life. This not only means that prayer and work, family and church, ministry and politics are all important, but that everything we do, whether great or small, is to be done for God's glory and the wellbeing of others. And since we can never be sure what will be important and significant in the lives of others, we need to be prayerful and discerning, asking the Spirit to guide us in everything we do. Above all, we need a heart willing to serve so that we are ever ready to do what we can and what we must.

THOUGHT: *Since we can never tell what ultimate fruit our actions will bear, we need simply to be obedient and leave the outcomes to God.*

Empowerment

'What is important is that the people. . . are able to walk with their own feet.'

Clodovis Boff

To empower people does not mean a leap to self-sufficiency. We cannot live apart from God's blessing, the sustenance of the earth, the nurture of family, the solidarity of the human community and the reality of the household of faith. Empowerment will always mean sharing, care, joining, solidarity and partnership. To empower people also does not necessarily mean arrival. It means struggle; journey; faith; courage. Empowerment simply means that the journey has begun, but that we are doing the walking. We are doing the visioning. We are doing the planning. We are making the decisions. We are mobilising the resources. And we are doing the work.

THOUGHT: *If we are able to act responsibly into our world, we can celebrate the fruit of our labours.*

Discerning obedience

'Since God does not expect blind obedience from God's children, Christians cannot even think of giving unconditional obedience to a worldly sovereignty.'

Allan Boesak

Obedience never works very well if it is motivated by fear or guilt. Obedience will be much more lasting if it springs from freedom and responsibility. The relevance of freedom has to do with making choices from a relatively free place. The importance of responsibility has to do with a recognition that this is the way I want to live because I believe it to be appropriate and relevant. My obedience to God can hardly be based on fear. Instead, it should be a considered and joyful response to the grace of God. My submission to all earthly authorities must be qualified in the light of my submission to the God who has saved me in Jesus Christ.

PRAYER: *Lord, may my obedience to you always spring from gratitude and may my obedience to all others spring from careful discernment.* Amen.

December

*People are also fundamentally
the same. Made in God's image,
we share in a common dignity,
a common humanity and
a common destiny.*

The blessing of prayer

'There are graces and there are experiences of
Christ in our lives that God gives us only during
prayer.'
                                              Segundo Galilea

For many of us, prayerfulness is not a particular
strength. Ministry or other forms of activism are
often much more dominant in our lives. This does
not necessarily mean that we regard activism as
purposeful and prayer as irrelevant. It may simply
be that we find prayer difficult. This may be true
even if we are highly intuitive and reflective people.
But we must attend to prayer, for everything else
that we do will be affected if we don't. In prayer,
we experience the sheltering presence of God. In
prayer, we experience God's forgiveness and
release from our bondages and fears. In prayer, we
hear God's wisdom and direction. And in prayer,
we be able to lay down those things that we hold
much too closely and tenaciously.

THOUGHT: *To remove prayer from our lives is like
filling up and damming a perennial, life-sustaining
spring of water.*

Non-violence

'Reconciliation is the ultimate aim of non-violence because non-violence holds not only for the absolute inviolability of the human person, both friend and enemy, but maintains that human beings are ultimately one family, brothers and sisters to each other.'

Niall O'Brien

People are fundamentally different: we can divide ourselves in terms of personality, gender, age, social status, race and religion. People are also fundamentally the same. Made in God's image, we share a common dignity, a common humanity and a common destiny. As such, we not only belong together, but we need to extend to others the same care that we would wish to bestow on ourselves. Therefore, we are constantly challenged to be involved with processes that produce peace and reconciliation, that build community, that give dignity to others, that empower others.

REFLECTION: *The fact that we belong to each other in the one human community is a fundamental reality that should constantly challenge the many distinctions that we so tirelessly seek to maintain.*

Simplicity

'The human way leads not from the simple to the complicated, but from the complicated to the simple.'

Arturo Paoli

We seem to have an innate propensity to make things difficult. This is true of our whole way of life; our technologies; our social systems; our institutions. It is also true of our theologies and our ways of being church. But we can also resist these forms of sophisticated 'madness'. Making things more complex does not necessarily mean that they become better. On the other hand, we can't wind back the clock to the supposed simplicity of a previous era. But things can be done in a different way. Instead of creating complex institutions of care, we can create communities of care. Instead of cathedrals, we can create house churches. Instead of organisations, we can create ministries.

THOUGHT: *Simplicity has nothing to do with being simplistic. Great ideas can find simple forms of expression and implementation.*

Counter culture

'There are times when God's plans and God's ways may go against the accepted norms and expectations of a given culture.'

Athena Gorospe

In God's purposes in history there runs a wonderful web of consistency. God affirms and transforms. God sustains existing structures, but also creates new ways of acting and being in the world. In God's strategy of engagement we see both a maintenance and a creative function. Christians are challenged to function in similar ways. We affirm what is good. We challenge what is evil. We gratefully accept what we have. We creatively explore better ways of operating and serving. In this dialectic of maintenance and creativity we need the gift of discernment, since we don't want to maintain what is essentially defective and we don't want to create what is inferior.

PRAYER: *Lord, we pray that your kingdom will be more and more manifest amongst us. Therefore, give us the gift of discernment to know your will and the courage to live it out.* Amen.

Sadness

'There is a real undertone of sadness to our whole life, sadness that we cannot love as we are loved.'

Thomas H. Green

Some say that the basic motif of life must be self-assertion. Others hold it is God's glorification. Still others claim that it is the service of others. Some say that a central feature of life is gratitude. Others believe it is power. But however we may wish to resolve these differing perspectives, we are all aware that contradictory emphases reside within each of us. We know how to be both glad and sad; strong and vulnerable; giving and witholding; purposeful and confused; certain and lacking direction. In the light of these conflicting realities, we so much need the grace of God and the help and encouragement of our friends.

THOUGHT: *While we may want to deny the shadow side of our life, we must face all of what we are in the light of God's grace.*

Bridge builders

'We are a bridge between God and our family. . .
our community. . . our place of work [and] between
God and our church. In short, we are a liaison between God and all life conditions through our
prayers of intercession and our service.'

Grace Eneme

The genius of life is not only creativity and the
creation of the new. It is also maintenance and the
nurturing of existing social realities and institutions.
Our world so much needs those who care enough
to maintain their relationships, families, churches
and institutions. This requires people who quietly
serve and who fervently pray. These are the ones
who put out brush fires before they become a
flaming holocaust. They are the ones working for
reconciliation and peace. These are the networkers
who help people to join together to work on common causes and projects. These are the glue in our
communities and social order.

THOUGHT: *Those who stand in the gap build bridges of
connectedness, pray and work for reconciliation and
peace. They are the true servants in our world.*

Meditative prayer

'Be still and become aware of your own breathing
. . . Close your eyes so that you can focus your attention
inwardly. . . . Allow the rhythm of your own breathing
to quiet your whole body and inner being. . . While
breathing in, lift up your heart to God while saying. . .
"Blessed be Yahweh". . . . While breathing out,
repeat to yourself the words, "My God, I praise
you". '

Judette A. Gallares

So many writings on spirituality talk about the
importance of reflection, meditation, solitude
and prayer. The reason for this is that coming to
inner quietness is so empowering and nurturing
for us. However, not only do we receive inward
peace; we are also renewed and refuelled for the
journey of life. But to come to the place of solitude
is difficult for us. We are distracted, busy and
often driven. Therefore, we should not be afraid
to use certain techniques to help us come to stillness. What works best will vary from person to
person, but do find ways to help you come to
meditative prayer!

Deuteronomy 8: 2–11   **December 8**

Stories

'When common people speak, they try to understand their experiences through parable, metaphors and stories, which keep them close to the concrete.'

Paulo Freire

Every individual, family, neighbourhood community, church, institution and nation has its particular experiences and social realities. Out of these realities emerge the stories and the myths. These are told and retold as part of our long memory and our communal identity. The power of these reflections lies in their ability to remind us of the tragedies, paradoxes and joys of life. They acknowledge the realities of abandonment and empowerment. Woven out of the fabric of life's experiences, they celebrate the goodness of

God and grieve over God's absences. And in their re-telling, we re-live their realities, looking in hope to a better future.

THOUGHT: *The ability to reflect and reminisce not only helps us make sense of the past, but empowers us for the future.*

Proverbs 30: 7–10   **December 9**

Forgetfulness

'Be careful. It seems to me that if God gave me a whole lot of things, I'd think I'd never need anything again. And so, I wouldn't think about God anymore.'

Olivia, a campesina

There is little virtue in little having. There is much danger in much having. But in the final analysis, the little or the much are not the real issues. What is much more fundamentally at stake is the overall direction of our life. One may have much and live generously towards others.

One may have little and be full of avarice. Those who have little should strive with God's help and blessing to improve their circumstances. Those who have much should live as responsible stewards under God's direction. Both, in the varied circumstances of their lives, need to depend on God and, in sharing life together in the community of believers, need to work towards partnership and sharing.

REFLECTION: *Since life is neither fair nor equal, the challenge facing all of us is to work towards a sharing that provides dignity and resources for all.*

Ephesians 4: 20–29   **December 10**

Empowerment

'If we wish to love the world in God's way, then we will freely choose to work in solidarity with "the lowly ones". Our aim will be to empower them to become agents of change in society.'

Donal Dorr

For empowerment to occur, the whole of life must be impacted. This involves not only a new sense of self-identity, but also a new set of common purposes. Empowerment seeks to build both the individual ego and the community. But empowerment also involves the social and economic realities of life. It involves the move beyond poverty and seeks to provide people with greater choices and opportunities to live with dignity. But there is also a profound spiritual dimension to the empowerment process, for the self cannot be built without reconciliation; and economic progress cannot prosper unless it is undergirded by moral values.

THOUGHT: *The long road to participation and empowerment is to be preferred to the short road of charity that may finally lead nowhere.*

Anger

'The anger of those who suffer most often carries within it a creativity imposed upon it by sheer necessity which needs to be incorporated into a theology given to social reconstruction.'

Charles Villa-Vicencio

Anger is a good emotion when we are angry for the right reasons. We should be angry in the face of injustice, particularly when others are affected. Anger in these situations is our assertion of life rather than a passive and debilitating resignation. And creative realities can come from such anger. The idea that anger is simply negative is a faulty notion. Anger can mobilise us to resist. It can galvanise us into action. It can move us to plan alternatives and to explore other options. The idea that good things can only come out of a placid reflection is nonsense. Good things can also emerge from a passionate commitment to change what is intolerable and unjust.

THOUGHT: *Anger can lead to a blinding, impulsive and explosive reaction. It can also move us to do something about that which we have accepted for far too long.*

No plan

'In his heart he carries faith, hope, great love, but he does not find a place for himself in this world.'

Carlos Mesters

Some are called to a life of contemplation. Others outwork their love for God and neighbour through an active apostolate. Yet others serve through marriage and a 'secular' vocation. Our service can take many differing forms. The one is not superior to the other. But our calling, vocation and service must not totally define us. We are more than what we do. Moreover, what we do must not totally possess us. We must live in the tension between involvement and disengagement and attachment and detachment. We are to be wholly involved in this world seeking its transformation, but at the same time we need to hold the things of this world lightly. Thus, while we have our face towards the world, we also long for the world to come.

REFLECTION: *A certain amount of detachment frees us for new directions and commitments.*

Life

'We are not born for pain or death. We are born for life and joy.'

Dom Helder Camara

God's purpose for us is not difficulty and pain, although these things occur in our lives; and in some people's lives more pain occurs than in others. We cannot and maybe should not try to puzzle out how and why this happens. We simply cannot understand why bad things happen to good people. While God's purpose is wholeness and blessing, this does not mean that God stands outside of our pain and struggle. God enters into both the joy and difficulties of our lives. In our pain, we can experience both God's comfort and that of our friends. But there is more. God so often brings good out of our difficulties and thus empowers us for the long journey of life and faith.

PRAYER: *Lord, in the midst of the joys and blessings of life help me to celebrate and to remember with gratitude all you have done. In the midst of pain, help me to trust you and commit my life into your care.* Amen.

Liberation through service

'Liberation is the fruit of a long process. There are steps that must be taken, and these begin with the praxis of the community itself. . . [it] must not be an oppressor, but a symbol of freedom of speech, of action, of participation.'

Leonardo Boff

God's liberative work stretches from the shattered dream of the garden of Eden to the consummation of all things in Christ in the new heaven and earth. While we don't know how close we are to that glorious end, we do know that a huge task still lies in front of us. There is the ongoing challenge of gospel proclamation to those who haven't heard and to those who need to hear again. There is the need to build a more just human community in the face of widespread poverty and oppression. And, undergirding these activities, is the challenge to build communities of believers that reflect the values of the kingdom of God. If these communities can reflect values of care, justice and empowerment, then the work of proclamation and transformation will be sustained.

Isaiah 56: 1–2   **December 15**

Dealing with causes

'You may have an army of bleeding hearts tending the sorrowful and the hungry and yet not see an end to the causes of hunger and thirst.'

Melba Maggay

We all know that the response of one person to the magnitude of human poverty and misery is like a drop in the ocean. We also know that charity can help in the immediate situation, but does nothing to alleviate long-term problems. Therefore, we need to commit ourselves to the long journey of social transformation, development and empowerment. But in seeking to deal with structural issues, we cannot make these only matters of the head while we close our hearts. Nor can we, in tackling the macro-issues, fail to respond to individuals in need.

THOUGHT: *Our projects can be ideologically and methodologically well thought out. But they may not achieve what we had hoped because the magic of love is not present.*

Mark 10: 35–45   **December 16**

Freedom

'Freedom. . . [means] that what I possess doesn't own me, so that what I possess doesn't hold me down, so that my possessions don't keep me from sharing and giving myself.'

Mother Teresa

God has endowed us with gifts, talents and many experiences. These have shaped our lives and have given us the ability to play certain roles and do certain tasks. In using our gifts, we develop and grow, make our small mark for good in the world and bless others. While we should celebrate and use our talents, we should not become overly attached to them. We are more than what we can do. And the blessings and affirmation we receive as a result of the use of our gifts should not possess us and blind us. Gifts are for giving. Blessings are for sharing. And our life is meant for loving service and celebration. Sadly, those who hold things for themselves alone will hardly be enriched and may well miss the very purpose of their existence.

THOUGHT: *True freedom will always express itself in generous service.*

Philippians 4: 4–9   December 17

Prayer

'The synthesis. . . being developed in Latin America is a synthesis of prayer *in* action, prayer *within* activity, prayer *with* the deed. What must be eliminated is a divorce between prayer on one side and action on the other side.'

Leonardo Boff

Prayer is prayer. It is not something else. And prayer is not action, just as social concern is not prayer. But life is an integrated whole. Spirituality belongs to the work of justice, just as prayer belongs to the work of social transformation. But the other way around is equally true. Community organising, mobilising people for action, building coalitions which will work for change, micro-economic development and other forms of community work need to be bathed in prayer just as much as our worship services. Prayer, therefore, is not simply an attitude that we carry in our hearts while we do our work. Prayer should be genesis and the end of all of our activity.

REFLECTION: *Prayer may not necessarily make everything we do more successful. But it does make it more pleasing to God and more sensitive to those we seek to serve.*

Christianity

'Christianity has become more difficult and, therefore, more necessary than ever.'

Hugo Assmann

In a final sense, Christianity is the great disturber. This is not to suggest that Christianity does not build cultural realities and social systems. It has done so in the past and will probably do so in the future. But there is also a prophetic impulse in Christianity. There is a restless movement towards truth and justice within Christianity, even while there may be a corresponding emphasis on stabilising social reality and political systems. This critical and transformative element will always be necessary. The call to acknowledge Christ's lordship over all of life, the call to radical discipleship and the call to work for kingdom values will always challenge us to transform the systems and structures we have created.

THOUGHT: *When Christianity remains true to the genius of the gospel, it will always be a radical force in the world.*

Crises

'The only way that a person or a group grows is by going through crises and unmasking themselves in order to live with more and more freedom.'

Segundo Galilea

We often think that our only task is to unmask the false values and ideologies of the world through communicating God's truth. But we also have some work to do on the home front. Our church traditions and our ecclesiastical structures can also mask the radical claims of the gospel. That is why gospel must take precedence over tradition and the egalitarian communities of the Pauline mission must challenge us to make our institutions into communities of care and empowerment. While we would like this transformative word to occur quietly and smoothly, it is often through difficulties and crises that our eyes are opened and we are prepared to consider new options and possibilities.

THOUGHT: *Traditions are good, but they also need to be renewed, particularly when they become dysfunctional.*

Sharing

'But a rich person that shares love has to share his goods, too. That's how he shows that he shares love.'

Mariíta, a campesina

The power of sharing lies not only in our ability to give some of our resources to others. While sharing may pose as a challenge for some, it is relatively easy for those who have much. However, there is more to sharing. It also involves the giving of ourselves in friendship and solidarity. To journey with people in their struggle for a life of dignity and wellbeing is a vital resource. And for people to know that we will be there for them in good and bad times involves a sharing that can truly empower. It should be obvious, however, that when we give ourselves we do not come empty handed.

THOUGHT: *Sharing need never be a burden when we make ourselves vulnerable enough to also receive.*

Lament

'In the prayer of lament, grief and anger belong to our full response to the situation [of oppression and injustice], for it helps us move towards solidarity.'

Judette Gallares

If we cannot grieve and we cannot be angry, we may well give way to that quiet, eroding sense of despair that destroys the fabric of our motivation and hope. To lament, therefore, is not an act of despair, but a sign of hope. To grieve our pain and losses is not a sign of defeat. It is an affirmation of life. And to be angry means that at the emotional level we are saying that these things ought not to be so. If we can turn our pain into prayer and turn our prayer into careful and constructive action, our threatening sense of despair can be avoided and we may well end up dancing to God's redemptive tune.

REFLECTION: *Face your pain. Grieve your pain. Learn from your pain. In this way, you don't waste your sorrows.*

All of life

'Liberation is an all-embracing process that leaves no dimension of human life untouched.'

Gustavo Gutiérrez

The God of the Bible is neither a legalist nor a tyrant, although the church throughout the ages has not always fully understood this fact. God, instead, is the God of grace and the God of liberation. God's transforming work moves us from where we are to where we ought to be. This involves us in a very long journey which affects every part of our lives: connectedness with God; inner wellbeing; families of care; communities of believers; empowering the poor; building more responsive institutions. God's liberative work is needed for every aspect of life lest what we have created falls into disrepair or becomes oppressive.

PRAYER: *Lord, may your renewing Spirit work in us and amongst us and through us and may your grace become manifest in all of our relationships.* Amen.

Realism

'There would be little hope for us if we met only praise and approval along our path: we might start to believe the good things we heard about ourselves and that is usually the beginning of the end.'

Dom Helder Camara

There is a certain blessing in self-forgetfulness. This has nothing to do with self-negation. I am not talking about making ourselves to be less than what we are because of some false humility or pietistic spirituality. We need to affirm ourselves and be aware of our gifts and abilities and to use these for the glory of God and the wellbeing of others. But we can't be focussed on the good we are doing. We are not doing things for others to make ourselves better. We simply do what we do because it is the good thing to do. We can then fall into forgetfulness, keeping no record or score-card.

PRAYER: *Lord, thank you for those who serve and bless me. Help me to bless others with joy and in simplicity.* Amen.

Conversion

'Conversion is a gift of God because it shows the way and invites us to enter the world of freedom, the world of life.'

Elsa Tamez

As the Mary Sisters of Darmstadt, Germany, emphasise: repentance is the joy-filled life. On the surface, this appears to be a strange statement. Conversion and repentance seem instead to be very sombre and possibly depressing experiences. There is some truth in this, but only because we are resisting the changes the Spirit of God is seeking to effect in our lives. When we stop rationalising and hesitating and take the plunge to turn from our wrongdoing and do what God asks of us, then we experience conversion and repentance as God's good gifts to us, bringing us life and joy.

REFLECTION: *Conversion turns away from that which is evil and destructive and turns to embrace what is good.*

My Lord and God!

'To acknowledge Jesus as our Lord and Saviour is only meaningful insofar as we try to live as he lived.'
Albert Nolan

The utter simplicity of the babe in a manger finds its historical culmination in a shameful death by crucifixion. Rather than human brutality frustrating the purposes of God, the Son of God defies death and invites us to receive his grace and embrace his cause. The post-Easter communities of believers shout and celebrate the Lordship of Christ and we are invited to join the party. But the members of these communities did more than celebrate. With passion and conviction, they set out to win the world's loyalty to their Master. That passion now blazes in the churches of the Third World and needs to be recaptured in the tired communities of believers of the First World. So let the magic continue: an innocent babe; an ignominious death; an amazing victory; a costly cause.

REFLECTION: *The embrace of faith links us to the cause of Christ to make God's kingly rule manifest in a broken world.*

Outsiders

'The correlation of the experience of "outsiders" with "insiders" involves a confrontation with the reality of a minority community in a dominant society. This minority community is aware of its alien status and yet is free to be itself and contribute to the wellbeing of all.'

Orlando Costas

Everywhere there are minority communities of believers. Their minority status may be due to theological, economic or ethnicity factors. Such communities, while running the risk of isolation, may well have experiences of faith and developed theological traditions that can enrich mainstream Christian churches. Those at the margins may well have ways of connecting with the Man of Galilee and enter his suffering and rejection that those who are located mainstream know little about. Since theological reflection involves the joining of the world of the Bible with our social world, those in minority positions may well have insights that the wider church needs to hear.

Mark 10: 17–22   **December 27**

Overly careful

'If we analyse every step we take as we are taking it, we will never get anywhere, and we may well stumble over our own feet.'

Thomas H. Green

Life is for living, loving, doing, acting, reflecting, worshipping and meditating. In both the active and reflective dimensions, we need to be balanced and discerning. But we also need to live in faith and hope. We therefore are challenged to live boldly and to take life in full stride. We can't afford to be overly careful in order to understand everything and get everything just right. Not only is this presumptuous and impossible; it may also result in our never risking anything. And a life lived to the full will always experience the agony of prayer, the risk of faith, the challenge to try again, the power to keep going in the face of odds and the 'madness' to dream the impossible dream.

THOUGHT: *Get the facts, analyse and plan. And pray and act in hope and faith.*

Prophet

'The poet plays his song to the living ones. But when he sings his song to the dead, he becomes a prophet.'

Rubem Alves

Our modern world is full of planners and programmers. These make things work, sometimes with deadly efficiency. But we also need people who put a bit of magic back into our world. The clown, the trickster, the seer, the songster, the artist, the poet. And we don't need these simply to provide a bit of comic relief. We need the seer and the poet to help us see what we should have seen, but dared not. In the process of unveiling and opening up of new possibilities, the artist and the poet take on the mantle of the prophet. They lilt us with the lullaby of long forgotten dreams and dare us to live again with boldness and hope.

REFLECTION: *If we can no longer soar and dream and hope, we are dead while we live. But if the magic is still there, we will live, no matter how great the difficulties and pain.*

2 Corinthians 3: 16–18　　　　　　**December 29**

God's grace

'No acceptance of God is possible on earth unless the Holy Spirit has prompted it; no effective sharing of God's life is possible unless the Son, Jesus Christ, has won it.'

Alfonso Aguirre

Everything else, no matter how great, beautiful or enchanting, can't bring us to true fulfilment, except the love and grace of God manifested in Jesus Christ. Whether it is the awesomeness of nature, the evocative power of music, the exhilarating joy of love, the stimulating impact of new ideas, the challenge of a new adventure, the audacity to do the impossible — none of these things of themselves can bring us to life's true meaning and adventure. That can only come when God becomes the centre out of which everything else can radiate. And God becomes the centre, not by strenuous adventure or gallant effort, but by the simplicity of faith, trust and surrender.

THOUGHT: *With God at the centre, the real adventure can begin.*

Completion

'Creation has been perfected through incarnation. It came closer to its aim, an aim which will be reached when the whole creation adds up to Christ.'

Ennio Mantovani

We live out of the richness and pain of the past and the challenges of the present. But we also live unto the future. For some, the future is bleak. Poverty, oppression and marginalisation don't look as if they will ever go away. For them, hope lies in the life to come. In some sense, this is true for all of us. Even when the future here may look bright and full of possibilities, difficulty and tragedy may befall us. And even if that does not happen, we all live with incompletion and imperfection. Therefore, we all need to hear the call of the future and pray for God to journey with us while we move to that which can never be taken away and will be perfect and complete.

PRAYER: *Lord, shelter and sustain us in the long journey of faith and bring us to your eternal kingdom through Jesus Christ, our Lord. Amen.*

What will they do?

'As we stepped into the street she asked me: "Will you remember me?" "Of course," I said, feeling a little hurt that she should ask this. "And will you tell people what you've seen here?" "Yes," I insisted, "you know I will." "And what will your people do?" she asked. "What will they *do*?"'

Daniel Santiago

We live in a broken world. Everywhere there are the signs of hope and the realities of decay. This state of affairs is hardly likely to change. The brokenness is often so apparent that the mending of our world seems an impossible task and we fall into despair or inactivity. But faith and courage can be given by God and thankfully received by us. Therefore, we dare to love, dare to dream and dare to act. Thus, the disturbing question faces each of us: Will we continue to be faithful and will we continue to act when so little seems to radically change in our needy world?

MEDITATION: *Identify what you should do, realising you can't do everything. And identify where your inner resources will come from and how you will act and respond. Then pray for the grace of perseverance.*

APPENDIX:

Alphabetical list of writers cited

AGUIRRE, Alfonso: president of the Asian Institute for Distance Education, Philippines.

ALVES, Rubem: Presbyterian sociologist and theologian teaching at the University of Campinao, Brazil.

ARELLANO, Luz Beatriz: Roman Catholic sister working in Nicaragua.

ARIAS, Mortimer: Protestant church worker among miners in Bolivia.

ARISTIDE, Jean-Bertrand: former parish priest and now president of Haiti.

ASSMANN, Hugo: Roman Catholic theologian teaching at the Methodist University, Piracicaba, Brazil.

ATEEK, Naim Stifan: Canon of St George's Cathedral in Jerusalem and pastor of its Arabic-speaking congregation.

BARREIRO, Alvaro: professor of theology at the Catholic University of Rio de Janeiro.

BAUTISTA, Ramon: Roman Catholic priest working in the Philippines.

BIDEGAIN, Ana Maria: lay Roman Catholic historian

who teaches at the University of the Andes in Bogota, Colombia.

BOESAK, Allan: former minister of the Dutch Reformed Mission Church in South Africa and president of the World Alliance of Reformed Churches.

BOFF, Clodovis: professor at the Catholic University in Sao Paulo and worker with the base ecclesial communities in Brazil.

BOFF, Leonardo: former Franciscan priest and seminary teacher in Petropolis, Brazil.

BOJAXHIV, Agnes: see Mother Teresa of Calcutta.

BONINO, José Míguez: dean of graduate studies at Union Theological Seminary, Buenos Aires, Argentina.

CAMARA, Dom Helder: former auxiliary bishop of Rio de Janeiro and later archbishop of Olinda and Recife in Northeast Brazil.

CASPERSZ, Paul: head of the centre for Social Research and Encounter in Kandy, Sri Lanka.

CINQUIN, Emmanuelle: Belgian nun of the Sisters of Our Lady of Sion who works among the ragpickers in the Cairo garbage dumps.

COE, Shoki: former principal of Taiwan Theological College, Taiwan.

COMBLIN, José: a Roman Catholic theologian, social critic and prolific author involved in pastoral work in Northeast Brazil.

COSTAS, Orlando: director of the Latin American

Evangelical Centre for Pastoral Studies in Costa Rica and dean of Andover Newton Theological School, USA, until his death.

DARDICHON, Francisco: religous worker from Bolivia.

D'ESCOTO, Miguel: Maryknoll priest and former foreign minister in the Nicaraguan government.

DEL PRADO, Consuelo: Roman Catholic sister from Peru.

DONDERS, Joseph: taught and served as student chaplain at the University of Nairobi, Kenya.

DORR, Donal: Roman Catholic missionary priest who has worked extensively in Africa and Latin America.

ELLACURÍA, Ignacio: formerly rector of Central American University, El Salvador. Martyred 16 November 1989.

ELWOOD, Douglas J.: professor of Theology and Ethics at the Silliman University Divinity School, Philippines.

ENEME, Grace: worker in the Presbyterian Church in Cameroun.

ESCOBAR, Samuel: Peruvian working in Argentina, he was president of the Latin American Theological Fraternity. He now teaches in the USA.

ESTRADA, Nelson: professor of New Testament at

Asian Theological Seminary, Metro Manila, Philippines.

FREIRE, Paulo: a well-known Brazilian educator.

GALDÁMEZ, Pablo: a pseudonym for a European priest who served as a missionary in El Salvador.

GALILEA, Segundo: pastoral worker in Santiago, Chile.

GALLARES, Judette A.: member of the Religious of the Cenacle in the Philippines.

GANDHI, M.K.: great Indian moral leader who used non-violent resistance to bring India to political freedom.

GANIBE, Josue: professor of pastoral theology at Asian Theological Seminary, Metro Manila, Philippines.

GILFEATHER, Katherine: social researcher who has worked in Chile.

GNANAKAN, Ken: theologian based in Bangalore, India and General Secretary of the Asia Theological Association.

GOMEZ, Fausto: professor at the University of Santo Tomas, Metro Manila, Philippines.

GOROSPE, Adonis: professor of theology at Asian Theological Seminary, Metro Manila, Philippines.

GOROSPE, Athena: professor of Old Testament at Asian Theological Seminary, Metro Manila, Philippines and leader of several Protestant communities.

GRANDE, Rutilio: Roman Catholic priest working in El Salvador who was killed in the late 1970s.

GREEN, Thomas H.: spiritual director at San Jose Seminary, Manila and professor of philosophy and theology at Ateneo de Manila University. He is a well-known writer on Christian spirituality.

GUTIÉRREZ, Gustavo: Roman Catholic theologian working among the urban poor in Lima, Peru.

KITAMORI, Kazoh: Japanese theologian.

LIBANIO, J.B.: professor of theology at the Pontifical Catholic University in Rio de Janeiro, Brazil.

LIM, David: leading evangelical Filipino theologian based in Metro Manila, Philippines.

MAGALIT, Isabelo: first Filipino president of Asian Theological Seminary, Metro Manila, Philippines.

MAGDAMO, Patricia L.: professor at Silliman University Divinity School, Philippines.

MAGGAY, Melba: leader of the Institute for Studies in Asian Church and Culture, Metro Manila, Philippines.

MANANZAN, Mary John: national chairperson of Gabriela and executive director of the Institute of Women's Studies, Metro Manila, Philippines.

MANGALWADI, Vishal: founder-director of the India-based Association for Comprehensive Rural Assistance.

MANTOVANI, Ennio: head of the Malanesian Institute for Pastoral and Socio-Economic Service, Papua New Guinea.

MATHEW, E.V.: was an eminent lawyer in Bangalore, India and a leader in the YMCA and SCM.

MATURA, Thaddée: New Testament scholar and exponent of Franciscan spirituality, currently living in the south of France.

MBITI, John: formerly professor of religious studies at Makerere University College, Uganda.

MESTERS, Carlos: Carmelite priest and biblical scholar working among the poor in Brazil.

MIRANDA-FELICIANO, Evelyn: well-known Filipino writer.

MOLEBATSI, Caesar: evangelical youth and church leader in Soweto, South Africa.

MORENO, Juan Ramón: a Jesuit priest, he worked in several Latin American countries and at the Central American University in San Salvador where he was murdered November 16, 1989.

MWOLEKA, Christopher: bishop of the church in Rulenge, Tanzania.

NACPIL, Emerito: former president and professor of Union Theological Seminary, Philippines.

NAKPIL, Carmen Guerrero: Filipino journalist.

NOLAN, Albert: former master general of the Dominican Order worldwide and researcher at the Institute of Contextual Theology in

Johannesburg, South Africa.

O'BRIEN, Niall: Columban priest who has worked for twenty years in the Philippines. He was imprisoned and later exiled during the Marcos dictatorship.

OKURE, Teresa: professor at the Catholic Institute of West Africa in Port Harcourt, Nigeria.

ORTIZ, Joel: president of Ebenezer Bible College and Seminary, Philippines.

OSTHATHIOS, Geevarghese Mar: Metropolitan of the Orthodox Syrian Church in Kerala, South India.

PADILLA, C. René: pastor of a Baptist Church in Buenos Aires and General Secretary of the Latin American Theological Fraternity.

PADOLINA, Priscilla: worker with the United Methodist Church in the Philippines.

PAOLI, Arturo: member of the Congregation of Little Brothers. Launched their first community in South America in Fortin Olmos, Argentina.

PAREDES, Tito: director of Centro Evangelico Missiologico Andino Amazonico, Latin America.

PICO, Juan Hernández: Jesuit priest who works in Managua, Nicaragua.

PIXLEY, Jorge: biblical scholar at Baptist Seminary, Managua, Nicaragua.

RAMODIBE, Dorothy: Administrative Secretary of the Institute of Contextual Theology in Braamfontien, South Africa.

RAYAN, Samuel: directs the Lumen Institute, Delhi, India.

ROMERO, Oscar: Roman Catholic archbishop of San Salvador, El Salvador martyred 24 March 1980.

SAMUEL, Vinay: Executive Director of the International Fellowship of Evangelical Mission Theologians, India.

SANTIAGO, Daniel: Roman Catholic priest who worked in a parish in the Archdiocese of San Salvador.

SEGUNDO, Juan Luis: international theological lecturer presently serving as chaplain to various groups in Uruguay.

SEPULVEDA, Juan: pastor, Servicio Evangelico Para El Desarollo, Chile.

SIN, Jaime: Cardinal of the Roman Catholic Church, Philippines.

SOBRINO, Jon: professor of philosophy and theology at the Universidad Jose Simeon Canas in El Salvador.

SONG, Choan-Seng: native of Taiwan and professor of theology at the Pacific School of Theology.

TAMEZ, Elsa: professor of biblical studies at the Seminario Biblico Latinoamericano in San José, Costa Rica.

TERESA, Mother: founder of the Missionaries of Charity. Started in 1950, the order is now a worldwide movement.

TORRES, Sergio: Roman Catholic priest from Chile and Executive Secretary of the Association of Third World Theologians.

TUTU, Desmond: formerly Archbishop of Cape Town and head of the Anglican Church in South Africa.

VILLA-VICENCIO, Charles: professor in the Department of Religious Studies, University of Cape Town.

WICKREMASINGHE, C. Laksham: formerly Anglican bishop of the Diocese of Kuranegala, Sri Lanka.

ZORRILA, Hugo: Colombian by birth and former professor at the Biblical Seminary, Costa Rica.

SOURCES OF TEXT QUOTES

January

1. *The True Church and the Poor*, Orbis, 1984, p.38
2. In N. Wolterstorff, *Until Justice and Peace Embrace*, Eerdmans, 1983, p.xi
3. *Truth and Social Reform*, Spire, 1989, p.98
4. In A. Beals, *Beyond Hunger*, Multnomah, 1985, p.72
5. *The Way of Living Faith: A Spirituality of Liberation*, Claretian, 1991, p.109
6. *The Meaning and Cost of Discipleship*, Bombay Urban Industrial League for Development, 1981, p.26
7. *Salvation and Liberation*, Claretian, 1985, pp.28-29
8. *Non-Violent Resistance*, Schoken, 1961, p.57
9. *The True Church and the Poor*, Orbis, 1984, p.45
10. *Bible of the Oppressed*, Orbis, 1982, p.68
11. *Through the Gospel with Dom Helder Camara*, Claretian, 1986, p.5
12. *Truth and Social Reform*, Spire, 1989, p.36
13. *We Drink From Our Own Wells*, Orbis, 1984, p.2
14. *The Way of Living Faith: A Spirituality of Liberation*, Claretian, 1991, p.110
15. *Introducing Liberation Theology*, Orbis, 1988, p.55
16. *The Meaning and Cost of Discipleship*, Bombay Urban Industrial League for Development, 1981, p.59
17. *The True Church and the Poor*, Orbis, 1984, p.45
18. In *Columbia Magazine*, 1988, p.8

19. *Bible of the Oppressed*, Orbis, 1982, pp.1-2
20. *Truth and Social Reform*, Spire, 1989, p.83
21. In S. Cassidy, *Good Friday People*, Darton, Longman and Todd, 1991, p.34
22. In *Third World Liberation Theologies: A Reader*, D.W. Ferm (ed.), Orbis, 1986, p.97
23. *Ibid*, p.257
24. *Theology for a Nomad Church*, Orbis, 1976, p.35
25. *Christians and Marxists: The Mutual Challenge to Revolution*, Hodder & Stoughton, 1976, p.40
26. *Charismatic Renewal and Social Action: A Dialogue* (with L.J. Suenens), Claretian, 1985, p.50
27. *The True Church and the Poor*, Orbis, 1984, p.37
28. *The Way of Living Faith: A Spirituality of Liberation*, Claretian, 1991, p.109
29. *The Meaning and Cost of Discipleship*, Bombay Urban Industrial League for Development, 1981, p.35
30. *Introducing Liberation Theology*, Orbis, 1988, p.48
31. In *Third World Liberation Theologies: A Reader*, D.W. Ferm (ed.), Orbis, 1986, p.95

February

1. *Theology for a Nomad Church*, Orbis, 1976, p.43
2. *A Question of Identity: Selected Essays*, Vessel, 1973, p.135
3. In *Third World Liberation Theologies: A Reader*, D.W. Ferm (ed.), Orbis, 1986, p.96
4. *Introducing Liberation Theology*, Orbis, 1988, p.50
5. *The Meaning and Cost of Discipleship*, Bombay Urban Industrial League for Development, 1981, p.54

6. *The True Church and the Poor*, Orbis, 1984, p.23
7. *Charismatic Renewal and Social Action: A Dialogue* (with L. J. Suenens), Claretian, 1985, p.14
8. *The Way of Living Faith: A Spirituality of Liberation*, Claretian, 1991, p.103
9. In *Columbia Magazine*, 1988, p.6
10. *Truth and Social Reform*, Spire, 1989, p.90
11. *In the Parish of the Poor: Writings from Haiti*, Orbis, 1990, p.24
12. *We Drink From Our Own Wells*, Orbis, 1984, p.15
13. *Charismatic Renewal and Social Action: a Dialogue* (with L. J. Suenens), Claretian, 1985, p.49
14. In *The Church and Women in the Third World*, J.C.B. & E.L. Webster (eds), Westminster, 1985, p.58
15. *Introducing Liberation Theology*, Orbis, 1988, p.4
16. *A Question of Identity: Selected Essays*, Vessel, 1973, p.135
17. In *Third World Liberation Theologies: A Reader*, D.W. Ferm (ed.), Orbis, 1986, p. 257
18. *One Heart Full of Love*, Servant, 1988, p.26
19. *A Flame for Justice* (with David Virtue), Lion, 1991, p.70
20. *The Meaning and Cost of Discipleship*, Bombay Urban Industrial League for Development, 1981, p.48
21. In G. Gutiérrez, *We Drink From Our Own Wells*, Orbis, 1984, p.145
22. *Theology for a Nomad Church*, Orbis, 1976, p.35
23. *Truth and Social Reform*, Spire, 1989, p.12
24. *We Drink From Our Own Wells*, Orbis, 1984, p.88
25. *In the Parish of the Poor: Writings from Haiti*, Orbis, 1990, p.3
26. *Gather Together in My Name*, Claretian, 1987, p.15
27. In Ernesto Cardenal, *The Gospel in Solentiname* (Vol. I), Orbis, 1982, p.5

28. In *Toward a Theology of People Power*, Douglas J. Elwood (ed.), New Day, 1988, p.70

March

1. *Spirituality of Hope*, Claretian, 1990, pp.38-39
2. *One Heart Full of Love*, Servant, 1988, pp.44-45
3. *Hoping Against All Hope*, Orbis, 1984, p.15
4. *We Drink From Our Own Wells*, Orbis, 1984, p.12
5. *Gather Together in My Name*, Claretian, 1987, p.27
6. *The Gospel in Filipino Context*, OMF Literature, 1987, p. 20
7. In *Directions in Theological Education*, L. Wanak (ed.), OMF Literature, 1994, p.31
8. *Voice of the Voiceless*, Orbis, 1985, p.70
9. In *African Theology en Route*, K. Appiah-Kubi & S. Torres (eds), Orbis, 1979, p.166
10. *First Steps in Discipleship*, OMF Literature, 1991, p.21
11. *Truth and Social Reform*, Spire, 1989, p.107
12. *One Heart Full of Love*, Servant, 1988, p.6
13. *Hoping Against All Hope*, Orbis, 1984, p.32
14. *Transforming Communities*, OMF Literature, 1992, p.12
15. In Ernesto Cardinal, *The Gospel in Solentiname* (Vol. II), Orbis, 1982, p.15
16. *A Flame for Justice* (with David Virtue), Lion, 1991, p.123
17. *Following Jesus*, Claretian, 1994, p.8
18. In *The Church and Women in the Third World*, J.C.B. & E.L. Webster (eds), Westminster, 1985, p.70
19. In *Third World Liberation Theologies:A Reader*, D.W.Ferm (ed.), Orbis, 1986, p. 106
20. *We Drink From Our Own Wells*, Orbis, 1984, p.77

21. In *What Asians Christians Are Thinking*, D.J. Elwood (ed.), New Day, 1978, p.199
22. *Voice of the Voiceless*, Orbis, 1985, p 74
23. *Walking on Thorns*, Eerdmans, 1984, p.18
24. In *Kairos: Three Prophetic Challenges to the Church*, R.M. Brown (ed.), Eerdmans, 1990, p.27
25. In *Third World Liberation Theologies: A Reader*, D.W. Ferm (ed.), Orbis, 1986, p.116
26. *Gather Together in My Name*, Claretian, 1987, p.45
27. *Following Jesus*, Claretian, 1994, p.15
28. *Hoping Against All Hope*, Orbis, 1984, p.3
29. *Transforming Communities*, OMF Literature, 1992, p.20
30. In *Evangelism and the Poor*, V. Samuel and C. Sugden (eds), Oxford Centre for Mission Studies, 1983, p.100
31. In *Third World Liberation Theologies: A Reader*, D.W. Ferm (ed.), Orbis, 1986, p.94

April

1. In *The New Face of Evangelicalism*, C. René Padilla (ed.), IVP, 1976, p.218
2. *Spiritual Discernment & Politics*, Orbis, 1982, p.27
3. In *Third World Liberation Theologies: A Reader*, D.W. Ferm (ed.), Orbis, 1986, p.105
4. In *Women and Religion*, M.J. Mananzan (ed.), Institute of Women's Studies, 1988, p.5
5. In *Living Theology in Asia*, J.C. England (ed.), SCM, 1981, p.180
6. *Charismatic Renewal and Social Action: A Dialogue* (with L.J. Suenens), Claretian, 1985, p.16
7. *Following Jesus*, Claretian, 1994, p.29

8. *Gather Together in My Name*, Claretian, 1987, p.36
9. In *Kairos: Three Prophetic Challenges to the Church*, R.M. Brown (ed.), Eerdmans, 1990 p.40
10. In *Third World Liberation Theologies: A Reader*, D.W. Ferm (ed.), Orbis, 1986, p.110
11. *Voice of the Voiceless*, Orbis, 1985, p.81
12. *One Heart Full of Love*, Servant, 1988, p.73
13. *We Drink From Our Own Wells*, Orbis, 1984, p.33
14. *First Steps in Discipleship*, OMF Literature, 1991, p.121
15. In *Faith Born in the Struggle*, D. Kirkpatrick (ed.), Eerdmans, 1988, p.180
16. *A Theology of Reconstruction*, Cambridge University Press, 1992, pp.252-253
17. In Ernesto Cardenal, *The Gospel in Solentiname* (Vol. III), Orbis, 1982, p.85
18. In *Through Her Eyes: Women's Theology from Latin America*, Elsa Tamez (ed.), Orbis, 1989, p.19
19. *Loving Jesus*, Servant, 1991, pp. 79-80
20. *The Holy Spirit and Liberation*, Orbis, 1989, p.6
21. *Hearts Burning*, Bookmark, 1990, p.11
22. *The Meaning and Cost of Discipleship*, Bombay Urban Industrial League for Development, 1981, p.57
23. *We Drink From Our Own Wells*, Orbis, 1984, p.27
24. *Introducing Liberation Theology*, Orbis, 1988, p.50
25. *Spiritual Discernment & Politics*, Orbis, 1982, p.20
26. In *Living Theology in Asia*, J.C. England (ed.), SCM, 1981, p.186
27. *Revolution Through Peace*, Harper & Row, 1971, p.37
28. *The Challenge of Popular Religiosity*, Claretian, 1988, p.52
29. *A Flame for Justice* (with David Virtue), Lion, 1991, p.21
30. *One Heart Full of Love*, Servant, 1988, p.8

May

1. *A Theology of Reconstruction*, Cambridge University Press, 1992, p.270
2. *In the Parish of the Poor: Writings from Haiti*, Orbis, 1990, p.12
3. *The Meaning and Cost of Discipleship*, Bombay Urban Industrial League for Development, 1981, p.63
4. *First Steps in Discipleship*, OMF Literature, 1991, pp.58-59
5. *Truth and Social Reform*, Spire, 1989, p.86
6. *We Drink From Our Own Wells*, Orbis, 1984, p.81
7. In Ernesto Cardenal, *The Gospel in Solentiname* (Vol. III), Orbis, 1982, p.54
8. *The True Church and the Poor*, Orbis, 1984, p.38
9. *Introducing Liberation Theology*, Orbis, 1988, p.50
10. *Spiritual Discernment & Politics*, Orbis, 1982, p.24
11. *Mission Between the Times: Essays on the Kingdom*, Eerdmans, 1985, p.192
12. In *Living Theology in Asia*, J.C. England (ed.), SCM, 1981, p.200
13. *Hoping Against All Hope*, Orbis, 1984, p.32
14. *The Way of Living Faith: A Spirituality of Liberation*, Claretian, 1991, p.110
15. *One Heart Full of Love*, Servant, 1988, p.129
16. *Hope and Suffering*, Collins, 1984, p.143
17. *A Journey of Liberation*, Claretian, 1989, p.15
18. In *Mission Trends No. 3: Third World Theologies*, G.H. Anderson & T.F. Stransky (eds), Paulist, 1976, p.96
19. *Walking on Thorns*, Eerdmans, 1984, p.31
20. *Basic Ecclesial Communities: The Evangelisation of the Poor*, Orbis, 1982, p.27

21. In *The Church in Response to Human Need*, V. Samuel & C. Sugden (eds), Eerdmans, 1987, p.69
22. *Transforming Society*, Regnum Lynx, 1994, p.19
23. In Ernesto Cardenal, *The Gospel in Solentiname*, (Vol. II), Orbis, 1982, p.46
24. *The Challenge of Popular Religiosity*, Claretian, 1988, p.61
25. *Hope and Suffering*, Collins, 1984, p.138
26. In G. Gutiérrez, *We Drink From Our Own Wells*, Orbis, 1984, p.105
27. *Spiritual Discernment & Politics*, Orbis, 1982, p.11
28. *Loving Jesus*, Servant, 1991, p.21
29. *Revolution Through Peace*, Harper & Row, 1971, p.1
30. *Christ in Philippine Context*, New Day, 1971, p.13
31. In *Mission Trends No. 3: Third World Theologies*, G.H. Anderson & T.F. Stransky (eds), Paulist, 1976, p.98

June

1. *One Heart Ful¹ of Love*, Servant, 1988, p.42
2. In *The Church in Response to Human Need*, V. Samuel and C. Sugden (eds), Eerdmans, 1987, p.79
3. In *With Passion and Compassion: Third World Women Doing Theology*, V. Fabella & M.A. Oduyoye (eds), Orbis, 1985, p.19
4. *Following Jesus*, Claretian, 1994, p.3
5. In Ernesto Cardenal, *The Gospel in Solentiname* (Vol. IV) Orbis, 1982, p.89
6. *Revolution through Peace*, Harper & Row, 1971, p.32
7. *Mission Between the Times: Essays on the Kingdom*, Eerdmans, 1985, p.193
8. *Spiritual Discernment & Politics*, Orbis, 1982, p.10

9. *We Drink From Our Own Wells*, Orbis, 1984, p.83
10. *Truth and Social Reform*, Spire, 1989, p.127
11. *In the Parish of the Poor: Writings from Haiti*, Orbis, 1990, p.14
12. *Hope and Suffering*, Collins, 1984, p.158
13. *A Journey of Liberation*, Claretian, 1989, p.29
14. In *Mission Trends No. 3: Third World Theologies*, G.H. Anderson & T.F. Stransky (eds), Paulist, 1976, p.107
15. *Walking on Thorns*, Eerdmans, 1984, p.23
16. *Basic Ecclesial Communities: The Evangelisation of the Poor*, Orbis, 1982, p.29
17. *Transforming Society*, Regnum Lynx, 1994, p.21
18. In Ernesto Cardenal, *The Gospel in Solentiname* (Vol. II), Orbis, 1982, p.52
19. In *With Passion and Compassion: Third World Women Doing Theology*, V. Fabella & M.A. Oduyoye (eds), Orbis, 1988, p.121
20. *Following Jesus*, Claretian, 1994, p.2
21. *Hope and Suffering*, Collins, 1984, p.150
22. *Gather Together in My Name*, Claretian, 1987, p.52
23. *The Poet, The Warrior, The Prophet*, SCM, 1990, p.34
24. In *Mission Trends No. 3: Third World Theologies*, G.H. Anderson & T.F. Stransky (eds), Paulist, 1976, p.123
25. *Conduct for Today*, OMF Literature, 1977, p.36
26. *A Pedagogy for Liberation* (with Ira Shor), Bergin & Garvey, 1987, p.5
27. *The Social Justice Agenda: Justice, Ecology, Power and the Church*, Claretian, 1993, p.126
28. *How to Work with People*, Claretian, 1988, p.29
29. *Spirituality of Hope*, Claretian, 1990, p.104
30. In Jon Sobrino, et al, *Companions of Jesus: The Jesuit Martyrs of El Salvador*, Orbis, 1990, p.102

July

1. *Church: Charism & Power,* SCM, 1985, p.17
2. In Ernesto Cardenal, *The Gospel in Solentiname* (Vol. III), Orbis, 1982, p.43
3. *The Way of Living Faith: A Spirituality of Liberation,* Claretian, 1991, p.81
4. *Revolution through Peace,* Harper & Row, 1971, p.29
5. *One Heart Full of Love,* Servant, 1988, p.1
6. *How to Work with People,* Orbis, 1988, p.14
7. *We Drink from Our Own Wells,* Orbis, 1984, p.23
8. *Come Down Zacchaeus: Spirituality & the Laity,* St Paul, 1988, p.11
9. In Ernesto Cardenal, *The Gospel in Solentiname* (Vol. III), Orbis, 1982, p.4
10. *The Christ of the Ignatian Exercises,* Orbis, 1987, p.52
11. *Transforming Society,* Regnum Lynx, 1994, p.85
12. *Spirituality of Liberation: Toward Political Holiness,* Orbis, 1988, p.x
13. *How to Share Jesus,* OMF Literature, 1985, p.27
14. *The Holy Spirit and Liberation,* Orbis, 1989, p.60
15. *Walking on Thorns,* Eerdmans, 1984, p.47
16. *Darkness in the Marketplace: The Christian at Prayer in the World,* St Paul, 1981, p.41
17. *Hoping Against All Hope,* Orbis, 1984, p.55
18. *Theology of a Classless Society,* Orbis, 1980, p.74
19. *Hearts Burning,* Bookmark, 1990, p.8
20. *Basic Ecclesial Communities: The Evangelisation of the Poor,* Orbis, 1982, p.30
21. *The Words of Desmond Tutu* (selected by Naomi Tutu), Newmarket Press, 1989, p.24
22. *Praying and Preaching the Sunday Gospel,* Orbis, 1988, p.5

23. *Gospel Radicalism: The Hard Sayings of Jesus*, Orbis, 1984, p.16
24. *To Share with God's Poor: Sister Among the Outcasts*, Harper & Row, 1982, p.16
25. *Theology of Christian Solidarity* (with Jon Sobrino), Orbis, 1985, p.67
26. In Felix B. Bautista, *Cardinal Sin and the Miracle of Asia*, Vera-Reyes, 1987, p.viii
27. In *Cloud of Witnesses*, Jim Wallis & Joyce Holliday (eds), Orbis, 1991, p.115
28. *Missions and Dialogue: Theory and Practice*, Leonardo N. Mercado & James J. Knight (eds), Divine Word, 1989, p.137
29. In *Mission Trends No. 3: Third World Theologies*, G.H. Anderson & T.F. Stransky (eds) Paulist, 1976, p.98
30. In *Third World Liberation Theologies: A Reader*, D.W. Ferm (ed.), Orbis, 1986, p.94
31. *The Holy Spirit and Liberation*, Orbis, 1989, p.1

August

1. *Transforming Society*, Regnum Lynx, 1994, p.97
2. In *Mission Trends No. 3: Third World Theologies*, G.H. Anderson & T.F. Stransky (eds), Paulist, 1976, p.119
3. In Ernesto Cardenal, *The Gospel in Solentiname* (Vol. III), Orbis, 1982, p.29
4. *The Poet, The Warrior, The Prophet*, SCM, 1990, p.8
5. *The Way of Living Faith: A Spirituality of Liberation*, Claretian, 1991, p.89
6. In *Living Theology in Asia*, J.C. England (ed.),

SCM,1981, p.216

7. *Spiritual Discernment & Politics*, Orbis, 1982, p.13
8. *One Heart Full of Love*, Servant, 1988, p.64
9. *The Holy Spirit and Liberation*, Orbis, 1989, p.6
10. In Jon Sobrino et al, *Companions of Jesus: The Jesuit Martyrs of El Salvador*, Orbis, 1990, p.110
11. *The Christ of the Ignatian Exercises*, Orbis, 1987, p.78
12. *Come Down Zacchaeus: Spirituality & Laity*, St Paul, 1988, p.20
13. In Ernesto Cardenal, *The Gospel in Solentiname* (Vol. II), Orbis, 1982, p.51
14. *Church: Charism & Power*, SCM, 1985, p.26
15. *Spirituality of Liberation: Toward Political Holiness*, Orbis, 1988, p.2
16. *How to Work with People*, Claretian, 1988, p.22
17. *Hoping Against All Hope*, Orbis, 1984, p.79
18. *Theology of a Classless Society*, Orbis, 1980, p.57
19. *Truth and Social Reform*, Spire, 1989, p.11
20. *New Eyes for Reading: Biblical and Theological Reflections from the Third World*, John S. Pobee & Bärbel von Wartenberg-Potter (eds), W.C.C., 1986, p.39
21. *Defenseless Flower: A New Reading of the Bible*, Claretian, 1990, p.25
22. *The Power of the Poor in History: Selected Writings*, SCM, 1983, p.55
23. *A Vacation with the Lord*, St Pauls, 1986, p.116
24. In Ernesto Cardinal, *The Gospel in Solentiname* (Vol. I), Orbis, 1982, p.37
25. *Spirituality of Hope*, Claretian, 1990, p.46
26. In Jon Sobrino et. al., *Companions of Jesus: The Jesuit Martyrs of El Salvador*, Orbis, 1990, p.155
27. *The Social Justice Agenda: Justice, Ecology, Power and the*

    Church, Claretian, 1993, p.106
28. In *Feminist Theology from the Third World: A Reader*,
    Ursula King (ed.), SPCK, 1994, p.320
29. In *Cloud of Witnesses*, Jim Wallis & Joyce Holliday
    (eds), Orbis, 1991, p.118
30. *Theology of Christian Solidarity* (with Jon Sobrino),
    Orbis, 1985, p.79
31. *Island of Tears, Island of Hope: Living the Gospel in a
    Revolutinary Situation*, Orbis, 1993, p. 78

September

 1. *Spirituality of Liberation: Toward Political Holiness*,
    Orbis, 1988, p.8
 2. *How to Share Jesus*, OMF Literature, 1985, p.65
 3. *The Christ of the Ignatian Exercises*, Orbis, 1987, p.52
 4. *Transforming Society*, Regnum Lynx, 1994, p.43
 5. *We Drink From Our Own Wells*, Orbis, 1984, p.25
 6. In Jon Sobrino et. al., *Companions of Jesus: The Jesuit
    Martyrs of El Salvador*, Orbis, 1990, p.107
 7. In Ernesto Cardenal, *The Gospel in Solentiname* (Vol.
    III), Orbis, 1982, p.64
 8. *How to Work with People*, Claretian, 1988, p.1
 9. *The Holy Spirit and Liberation*, Orbis, 1989, p.39
10. *Hearts Burning*, Bookmark, 1990, p. 13
11. *Darkness in the Marketplace: The Christian at Prayer in
    the World*, St Paul, 1981, p.45
12. *Hoping Against All Hope*, Orbis, 1984, p.82
13. *Church: Charism & Power*, SCM, 1985, p.19
14. *Theology of a Classless Society*, Orbis, 1980, p.105
15. *The Meaning and Cost of Discipleship*, Bombay Urban

Industrial League for Development, 1981, p.18

16. In *Conflict and Context: Hermeneutics in the Americas*, Mark Lau Branson & C. René Padilla (eds), Eerdmans, 1986, p.86
17. In *Phronesis*, Vol. 2, No. 2, 1995, p.18
18. In Ernesto Cardenal, *The Gospel in Solentiname* (Vol. II), Orbis, 1982, p.167
19. *One Heart Full of Love*, Servant, 1988, pp.5-6
20. *The Words of Desmond Tutu* (selected by Naomi Tutu), Newmarket Press, 1989, p.65
21. In *The Church in Response to Human Need*, Vinay Samuel & Christopher Sugden (eds), Eerdmans, 1987, p.62
22. In José Cristo Rey Gardia Paredes, *Latin American Theologians on Religious Life*, Claretian, 1989, p.44
23. In *Mission Trends No. 3: Third World Theologies*, G.H. Anderson & T.F. Stransky (eds), Paulist, 1976, p.92
24. *Praying and Preaching the Sunday Gospel*, Orbis, 1988, p.124
25. *Voice of the Voiceless*, Orbis, 1985, p.68
26. *Basic Ecclesial Communities: The Evangelisation of the Poor*, Orbis, 1982, p.32
27. *One Heart Full of Love*, Servant, 1988, p.2
28. *Mission Between the Times: Essays on the Kingdom*, Eerdmans, 1985, p.141
29. *Truth and Social Reform*, Spire, 1989, p.126
30. *Spiritual Discernment & Politics*, Orbis, 1982, p.102

October

1. *The Poet, The Warrior, The Prophet*, SCM, 1990, p.3

2. *Transforming Society*, Regnum Lynx, 1994, p.71
3. *How to Share Jesus*, OMF Literature, 1985, p.75
4. *A Question of Identity: Selected Essays*, Vessel, 1973, p.135
5. *Voice of the Voiceless*, Orbis, 1985, p.95
6. *The Words of Desmond Tutu* (selected by Naomi Tutu), Newmarket Press, 1989, p.28
7. In Ernesto Cardenal, *The Gospel in Solentiname* (Vol. III), Orbis, 1982, p.157
8. *The Good News of Justice: Share the Gospel, Live Justly*, Herald, 1988, p.38
9. *A Vacation with the Lord*, St Pauls, 1986, p.44
10. *A Pedagogy for Liberation* (with Ira Shor), Bergin & Garvey, 1987, p.118
11. *Restoring the Fallen: The Practice of Church Discipline* (with Isabelo Magalit), OMF Literature, 1994, p.8
12. In *New Eyes for Reading: Biblical and Theological Reflections by Women from the Third World*, John S. Pobee & Bärbel von Wartenberg-Potter (eds), WCC, 1986, pp.30-31
13. *The Way of Living Faith: A Spirituality of Liberation*, Claretian, 1991, p.148
14. *The Holy Spirit and Liberation*, Orbis, 1989, p.54
15. *We Drink from Our Own Wells*, Orbis, 1984, p.3
16. *Through the Gospel with Dom Helder Camara*, Claretian, 1986, p.32
17. In *Conflict and Context: Hermeneutics in the Americas*, Mark Lau Branson & C. René Padilla (eds), Eerdmans, 1986, p.84
18. *To Share with God's Poor: Sister Among the Outcasts*, Harper & Row, 1982, p.41
19. *Praying and Preaching the Sunday Gospel*, Orbis, 1988, p.47

20. *Gather Together in My Name: Reflections on Christianity and Community*, Claretian, 1987, p.40
21. *Island of Tears, Island of Hope: Living the Gospel in a Revolutionary Situation*, Orbis, 1993, p.187
22. *A Pedagogy for Liberation* (with Ira Shor), Bergin & Garvey, 1987, p.55
23. In Ernesto Cardinal, *The Gospel in Solentiname* (Vol. I), Orbis, 1982, p. 191
24. *Walking on Thorns*, Eerdmans, 1984, p.40
25. In *Mission Trends No. 3: Third World Theologies*, G.H. Anderson & T.F. Stransky (eds), Paulist, 1976, p.24
26. *Church: Charism and Power*, SCM, 1985, p.128
27. *Spiritual Discernment & Politics*, Orbis, 1982, p.78
28. *Transforming Society*, Regnum Lynx, 1994, p.83
29. In *All Together in One Place*, Harold D. Hunter & Peter D. Hocken (eds), Sheffield Academic Press, 1993, p.56
30. *Faith of a People*, Orbis, 1986, p.21
31. *The Words of Desmond Tutu* (selected by Naomi Tutu), Newmarket Press, 1989, p.73

November

1. In Jon Sobrino et.al, *Companions of Jesus: The Jesuit Martyrs of El Salvador*, Orbis, 1990, p.118
2. In *Through Her Eyes: Women's Theology from Latin America*, Elsa Tamez (ed.), Orbis, 1989, p.148
3. *One Heart Full of Love*, Servant, 1988, p.127
4. *A Journey of Liberation*, Claretian, 1989, p.31
5. *Transforming Society*, Regnum Lynx, 1994, p.93
6. *Gather Together In My Name: Reflections on Christianity and Community*, Claretian, 1987, pp.116–117

7. *Island of Tears, Island of Hope: Living the Gospel in a Revolutionary Situation*, Orbis, 1993, p. 178
8. *The Words of Demond Tutu* (selected by Naomi Tutu), Newmarket Press, 1989, p. 91
9. In *Phronesis*, Vol. I, 1994, p.51
10. In *New Eyes for Reading: Biblical and Theological Reflections by Women from the Third World*, John S. Pobee & Bärbel von Wartenburg-Potter (eds.) WCC, 1986, p.51
11. *The Way of Living Faith: A Spirituality of Liberation*, Claretian, 1991, p.83
12. *Images of Faith: Spirituality of Women in the Old Testament from a Third World Perspective*, Claretian,1992, p.115
13. *A Pedagogy for Liberation: Dialogues on Transforming Education* (with Ira Shor), Bergin & Garvey, 1987, p.185
14. In Ernesto Cardenal, *The Gospel in Solentiname* (Vol. I), Orbis, 1982, p.107
15. *The Social Justice Agenda: Justice, Ecology, Power and the Church*, Claretian, 1991, p.147
16. *A Vacation with the Lord*, St Pauls, 1986, p.132
17. *Church: Charism & Power*, SCM, 1985, p.159
18. *Transforming Society*, Regnum Lynx, 1994, p.79
19. *One Heart Full of Love*, Servant, 1988, p.36
20. *Liberation Theology & Christian Liberation*, University of Santo Tomas, 1987, p.60
21. *Kingdom Concerns: A Theology of Mission Today*, IVP, 1993, p.183
22. *Jesus before Christianity: The Gospel of Liberation*, Darton, Longmann & Todd, 1977, p.32
23. *Justice and only Justice: A Palestinian Theology of Liberation*, Orbis, 1989, p.154

24. *Third-Eye Theology* (Revised Edition), Orbis, 1979, p.185
25. *Revolution through Peace*, Harper & Row, 1971, pp.142-143
26. *The Truth Shall Make You Free: Confrontations*, Orbis, 1990, p.138
27. *Hearts Burning*, Bookmark, 1990, p.18
28. *Faith on the Edge*, Harper & Row, 1989, p.157
29. *How to Work with People*, Claretian, 1988, p.13
30. *Walking on Thorns*, Eerdmans, 1984, p.60

December

1. *Following Jesus*, Claretian, 1994, p.50
2. *Island of Tears, Island of Hope: Living the Gospel in a Revolutionary Situation*, Orbis, 1993, p.102
3. *Gather Together in My Name: Reflections on Christianity and Community*, Claretian, 1987, p.166
4. In *Phronesis*, Vol. 2, No. 2, 1995, p.39
5. *A Vacation with the Lord*, St Pauls, 1986, p.65
6. In *New Eyes for Reading: Biblical and Theological Reflections by Women from the Third World*, John S. Pobee & Bärbel von Wartenberg-Potter (eds), WCC, 1986, p.31
7. *Images of Faith: Spirituality of Women in the Old Testament from a Third World Perspective*, Claretian, 1992, p.192
8. *A Pedagogy for Liberation: Dialogues on Transforming Education* (with Ira Shor), Bergin & Garvey, 1987, p.150
9. In Ernesto Cardenal, *The Gospel in Solentiname* (Vol. I), Orbis, 1982, p.212
10. *The Social Justice Agenda: Justice, Ecology, Power and the Church*, Claretian, 1991, p.174

11. *A Theology of Reconstruction*, Cambridge University Press, 1992, p.279

12. *A Journey of Liberation*, Claretian, 1989, p.10

13. *Through the Gospel with Dom Helder Camara*, Claretian, 1986, p.139

14. *Church: Charism & Power*, SCM, 1985, p.137

15. *Transforming Society*, Regnum Lynx, 1994, p.17

16. *One Heart Full of Love*, Servant, 1988, p.53

17. *Faith on the Edge*, Harper & Row, 1989, p.84

18. In *Faith Born in the Struggle for Life*, Dow Kirkpatrick (ed.), Eerdmans, 1988, p.37

19. *Following Jesus*, Claretian, 1994, p.95

20. In Ernesto Cardenal, *The Gospel in Solentiname* (Vol. I), Orbis, 1982, p.174

21. *Images of Faith: Spirituality of Women in the Old Testament from a Third World Perspective*, Claretian, 1992, p.79

22. *We Drink from our Own Wells*, Orbis, 1984, p.2

23. *Revolution through Peace*, Harper & Row, 1971, p.66

24. *Bible of the Oppressed*, Orbis, 1982, p.81

25. *Jesus before Christianity: The Gospel of Liberation*, Darton, Longman and Todd, 1977, p.139

26. In *Struggles for Solidarity: Liberation Theologies in Tension*, L.M. Getz & R.O. Costa (eds), Fortress, 1992, p. 68

27. *Weeds Among the Wheat: Discernment — Where Prayer and Action Meet*, Ave Maria, 1984, p.148

28. *The Poet, The Warrior, the Prophet*, SCM, 1990, p.135

29. *Christ, Layman: Towards Renewal of Theology for the Laity in the Church*, Asia's Social Institute, 1986, p. 107

30. In *Mission & Dialogue: Theory and Practice*, L.N. Mercado & J.J. Knight (eds), Divine Word, 1989, p. 43

31. *The Harvest of Justice: The Church of El Salvador Ten Years after Romero*, Paulist, 1993, p.192

11. *The Mirror* (from the book *Cambridge University Press* 1997, p.23)
12. A. Johnson, *Liberalism*, Carcanet, 1988, p.10
13. *Through the Looking with Dark Humour*, Carcanet, 1986, p.199
14. *Charlie Carcanet & Rope*, SCM, 1997, p.197
15. *Transforming society*, Penguin Books, 1991, p.137
16. *Out (Heart of Barn Servant*, 1983, p.156
17. ibid, *on the Edge*, Harper & Row, 1961, p.18
18. *to Point Light in the Struggle for Law*, Eds Kirkpatrick (ed.), *reference*, 1983, p.27
19. *Edge of Time*, Carcanet, 1997, p.45
20. *to Carolyn Cocker, The Church in Revolution* (Vol 11), Orbis, 1982, p.163
21. *Imagining the Spiritual Life Now in the Old Testament*, from First World Transition*, Carcanet, 1983, p.99
22. *We Are What Don't say*, Wade Orbis, 1984, p.22
23. *Sorting a message home*, Harper & Row, 1979, p.62
24. *Bible of the Deceased*, Orbis, 1983, p.61
25. *Jesus before Christianity*, The Catholic Revolution, Darton, Longman and Todd, 1977, p.66
26. *to Struggles for Spirit of Liberation Theology*, in *Tension, SAT, Geoffrey Chapman* (eds), Fortress, 1972, p.38
27. *Words Along the Ward Disarmament*, Tilney Paper and Sumner Men, Ave Maria, 1985, p.160
28. *The Paul Tillich Warner, the greater power*, 1977, p.188
29. *Cross Language Power—Kenneth J. Davies, the Larry little Charity, Auld's*, article, volume 16(3), p.177
30. *Thesaurus Gelhoff's Theological Studies*, Abhandlungen & J.J. Koogle (eds), *Doctor Word*, 1963, p.80
31. *The domain for faith, The Church of England Trust*, source to Koonty Faithful, 1989, p.102